The Children (Scotland) Act 1995
Regulations and Guidance
Volume 3

THE SCOTTISH OFFICE

The Children (Scotland) Act 1995 Regulations and Guidance

Volume 3
Adoption and Parental Responsibilities Orders

Social Work Services Group

Printed in Scotland for The Stationery Office Limited by CC No. 37907 C20 9/97

Contents

Volume 3: Adoption and Parental Responsibilities Orders

Guidance

CHAPTER I

Adoption

Introduction

1.   The Children (Scotland) Act 1995 introduced a number of amendments to the Adoption (Scotland) Act 1978. These reflected the main conclusions of the Adoption Law Review which indicated confidence in the legislation and a need for only limited change. The amendments to the 1978 Act - which is maintained as the primary piece of legislation on adoption - include a duty on courts and adoption agencies to regard the need to safeguard and promote the welfare of the child throughout his or her life as the paramount consideration. This guidance embraces the 1978 Act as amended, and also the principal piece of subordinate legislation, The Adoption Agencies (Scotland) Regulations 1996. Any margin references to sections or Regulations, unless otherwise indicated, refer to the above Act or Regulations.

2.   Since the 1978 Act came into force, the number of children placed for adoption by adoption agencies has fallen but the levels of difficulty and disability of the children placed have grown considerably. Services which were predominantly designed to find adoptive placements for healthy babies have changed and developed into family finding services for some of the most disadvantaged children in Scotland. At the same time, and partly as a consequence, a greater need for post adoption services for adopted children and adults, adoptive parents and birth parents has been recognised.

3.   There are two categories of adoption agency

- local authorities

- approved adoption societies.

All local authorities are obliged to provide an adoption service in their area and such services should be included in their children's services plan. An adoption society may either provide the full range of adoption services or only some of the services. An adoption society must be approved by the Secretary of State for those services it plans to provide. *Section 1* *Section 3*

4.   Local authority adoption agencies have a duty to meet the needs of children who have been or may be adopted, parents and guardians of such children and those who have adopted, or may adopt, a child. They must have arrangements in place for assessing children and prospective adopters, placing children for adoption and post-placement support. Post-placement support now specifically includes counselling and assistance to children who have been adopted and people who have adopted them, as well as counselling for anyone else with problems about adoption. In carrying out these duties, local authorities must act in conjunction with approved adoption societies and may allow such societies to carry out some of their duties. *Section 1*

The responsibility for maintaining the adoption service, however, lies with the local authority.

Placing Children for Adoption

Statutory requirements

Section 6   5.   Adoption agencies in making any decision in relation to the adoption of a child must

- regard the need to safeguard and promote the welfare of the child throughout his or her life as their paramount consideration

- so far as is practicable take account of the views of the child, if the child wants to express them, and in doing so take account of the child's age and maturity (any child who is twelve or over should be presumed capable of having a view, but many younger children will also have the maturity to express a view)

- so far as is practicable take account of the child's religious persuasion, racial origin, and cultural and linguistic background

Section 7   • so far as is practicable take account of the wishes of a child's parents or guardians about the religious upbringing of the child

Section 6A   • consider for every child whether adoption is in the best interests of that child or whether there is a better practicable alternative.

Regulation 11(2)(b)   Where also an adoption panel recommend that contact with parents should continue, they must provide a written record of the reasons why adoption is recommended rather than an alternative course of action.

6.   Where it has been decided that adoption is the best course for a child, the adoption agency must decide on the most appropriate route to adoption. An application may be made to free the child for adoption followed by an adoption application by the prospective adopters. Alternatively the agency may choose to *Section 18*   pursue an adoption application only. A freeing application can only be made by a local authority adoption agency. If a freeing petition is granted, all the parental responsibilities and rights in relation to the child are transferred from the birth parents to the adoption agency. Before a child can be freed for adoption, the court has to be satisfied that the child has either been placed for adoption with prospective adopters, or is likely to be placed.

Section 23   7.   Where an adoption agency has placed a child, and the prospective adopters raise an adoption petition in court, the agency which placed the child has a duty to prepare a report for the court about the suitability of the applicants, and other relevant issues to do with the child and the proposed adoptive parents.

The planning process

8.   If the local authority has ruled out the possibility of the child returning to live with the birth parents and placement with the extended family is unable to meet the needs of the child, alternative plans need to be made without delay. The agency should consider the available options and seek legal advice. When the chosen option is adoption, there should be clearly defined time-scales for completion of the reports on the child for the adoption panel and the court.

9.   A thorough assessment of the child's needs is necessary, both for the decision-making process and for preparing court reports. This should take into account information from present and previous carers and other professionals who know the child, for example, the class teacher, a health visitor, the medical adviser or an educational psychologist.

10.   The racial, religious, cultural and linguistic aspects of the child's heritage should be identified. Specialist advice may need to be sought where those planning for the child do not share the child's background and may lack knowledge or understanding of his or her heritage. Generally, it is easier for a child to feel knowledgeable, confident and comfortable about his or her racial, religious, linguistic and cultural background if this is shared by his or her adopters and efforts should be made to recruit a sufficiently diverse group of adopters to meet the varied needs of the children requiring adoption. In order to meet a child's particular needs, it may sometimes be necessary to seek a family through an inter-agency placement.   *Section 6*

11.   Occasionally, because all the options for obtaining an ideal placement have been exhausted and the wait for a placement would be detrimental to the child, a placement which does not completely match the child's heritage will need to be made. It is important in any such placement that the family is, or is helped by the agency to become, knowledgeable about the child's heritage, is prepared to maintain links with the child's community and is able to help the child deal effectively with any prejudice he or she may encounter.

12.   The needs of each child in a family group and the quality of the relationships between them should be assessed. The effect of past experiences needs to be taken into account. Where siblings are separated in their current placements, agencies should promote regular contact between them in order to maximise the chances of sustaining or improving existing bonds. There is research evidence that when children are placed with siblings, placements are more likely to have positive outcomes. Wherever possible, therefore, except where it has been explicitly identified that siblings need to be placed separately due to conflicting individual needs, steps should be taken to secure an adoptive placement which can meet the needs of all the children in a family group together. Specific recruitment or an inter-agency placement may increase the possibility of keeping siblings together.

Working with the child

13.   Careful preparation of children can maximise the chance of success of a placement. The child's views should be well represented at each stage in the process. Children of twelve or over must give consent to adoption but if younger children who are mature enough to have any understanding of their situation are not committed to the plan to place them for adoption, the chances of the placement disrupting will increase. Agencies should find ways to help children feel that they are heard and their opinion considered and respected.

14.   Ascertaining the child's wishes and feelings is linked to helping the child understand past events in his or her life and to the social worker reaching an understanding of the child's views. Direct work with the child needs to be underpinned by a thorough understanding of child development. Social workers should consider the implications of developmental delay for the child. It is important to gauge the pace at which the child should be prepared for the possibility of an

adoptive placement. Where age or other attributes of the child make it uncertain whether it will be possible to find an adoptive placement, more general preparation for a permanent placement, rather than specifically an adoptive placement, may be helpful.

15.   Social workers should develop a variety of approaches to working with children and should involve carers as fully as possible. Such work should be seen as a process which will be continued by the adoptive parents and not as something which is completed when, for example, a life story book is finished. Groupwork can be an effective way of preparing children, helping them to understand how an adoptive family is found for them and giving a safe place to talk about how they feel with other children who are in a similar position. A group should not be held at too early a stage for the child. Agencies may consider running groups jointly so that they have enough children to participate.

16.   Preparation work with children requires specific skills and training, and support for workers and carers is essential. Specialist knowledge, particularly about children not of the same racial or cultural background as the worker, should be available.

The linking process

17.   Linking a child with prospective adopters is a sensitive process. In considering arrangements to make links between children and families there should be a balance between giving the child and prospective family enough information about each other to enable them to decide whether or not they feel they have enough in common to allow a link to go ahead. At the same time care should be taken that they do not become so committed to each other that they are distressed if they are not the chosen child or family.

18.   Agencies should consider having a pre-linking meeting prior to the adoption panel, particularly in situations where more than one family is being considered for a child or where a child has complex needs. This meeting would be attended by the social workers for the child and for potential families and would allow discussion of the child's particular needs. Such a meeting should not pre-empt the recommendation of the adoption panel. A minute of the meeting or a copy of a report outlining why a particular link or links might be appropriate should be given to the adoption panel.

Regulation 19(1)

19.   The support which will be available to the family, both post placement and post adoption, should be discussed with them as part of the linking process since their ability to parent a particular child may be directly affected by the level of support which will be available. Once the linking has been agreed, the family should be given a copy of the details in writing so that they will know who will be involved, what their role will be, what services will be available and what will be expected of the family, for example in terms of facilitating contact. They should be told that the arrangements can be renegotiated as appropriate.

Introduction of the child and adopters

20.   When the link of a family with a child has been approved by the agency, information about the family should be provided for the child such as photographs, albums, or videos. It is important for current carers to meet the prospective family

before introductions start. This enables the prospective family to receive information about the child and to become familiar with the child's routine.

21.   The introductory period should be planned in advance in a forum which involves the prospective adopters, the carers and the relevant social workers. The pace of introductions is very important and everyone should feel comfortable with what is planned so that they feel able to say if things are going too fast or too slow.

22.   A number of factors will influence the length and intensity of the introduction. For instance the age and development of the child, his or her particular needs and understanding of the process, and whether siblings are being placed together. Arrangements need to be monitored and reviewed to take account of the child's and prospective adopters' views and reactions. Both the child and the adopters may need reassurance that it is appropriate to express any negative reactions. It is important that an introduction does not gain an unstoppable momentum which prevents doubts or concerns being addressed. There should not be avoidable delays.

23.   The carers for the child will be experiencing emotions about the child leaving as well as making practical arrangements and may also have to cope with some difficult behaviour from the child as he or she adjusts to the new family. They may need considerable support from the agency during this process.

24.   The decision about when the child should move to his or her new family should be made when all those involved are satisfied that the child is sufficiently ready to move. The child will need time to say his or her farewells to those who have been important in the previous placement. The appropriateness of continuing contact with carers should be considered.

Financial assistance

25.   In some instances adopters make a significant financial outlay at the point of placement. They may need to purchase furniture, additional bedding, toys and clothing. Some adopters, who are taking large sibling groups or a child with a disability, may require alterations to their homes or a larger or adapted vehicle. Adoption agencies should consider whether financial assistance is necessary.

26.   Adoption agencies may consider the payment of legal expenses incurred by the adopters in pursuing an adoption order. Adopters need to know prior to the placement what legal expenses, if any, they will have to meet. The question of payment of legal expenses is a separate issue from any consideration of eligibility for adoption allowances and one should not preclude the other. Agencies may wish to consider whether the adoption panel has a role to play in decisions about legal expenses.

Making and monitoring the placement

27.   An adoption agency is required to visit within one week of the child being placed with prospective adopters and thereafter on such other occasions as the agency considers necessary until the adoption order is made. If the adopters or child request an additional visit, one should normally be made unless the request is clearly unreasonable. The settling in period is crucial to the success of the placement and even adopters of babies will have mixed emotions and practical difficulties to cope   *Regulation 19(2)*

with. For instance they may find that they do not bond immediately with the child, or that they are exhausted by a baby who cries a great deal. Regular visits, particularly to adopters of older children, will usually be necessary until the time that the adoption order is made. The aims of the visits should be

- to safeguard the child's welfare

- to monitor the progress of the placement including, where applicable, any contact arrangements

- to provide support to the prospective adopters

There should be a written report made of these visits.

28.   At the start of a placement, it is desirable that the child and the adopters have separate social workers as both need support. The child should have regular contact with a social worker whom he or she knows even if the placement is made a long distance away. This social worker should talk to the child on his or her own on a regular basis. As the placement progresses, there may no longer be a need for more than one social worker. A decision to withdraw should be made after careful discussion with all concerned.

29.   The decision about when to lodge the petition in court to adopt the child should be made by the adopters in consultation with the agency. It is important that the adopters and the child, if old enough to be involved in the decision, feel that they are ready to pursue this step, without pressure to do so from the agency.

Services for Birth Parents

Birth parents' requirements

Section 1(1)(b)   30.   Birth parents whose children have been placed for adoption are entitled to a service in their own right. Some birth parents who have given a child up for adoption may experience feelings of guilt, loss and low self-esteem for many years. For others, it has a profound impact on their mental health. This applies equally to those who cease to be a child's parents through a contested adoption procedure which identifies their short-comings as parents. Agencies, therefore, should ensure a service is available for birth parents both before and after their child is adopted to help them deal with such difficulties. Birth parents may feel inhibited from approaching the agency which placed their child for adoption for such a service. This is an area where partnerships between local authorities or between local authorities and adoption societies may be fruitful. These services will be most likely to meet birth parents' requirements if, where possible, birth parents are consulted about the services they consider they will need.

Written information

31.   Agencies should make written information available to birth parents which describes their adoption policy and practice, the services that are available to birth parents both up to the time of adoption and subsequently and, in the case of voluntary agencies, any religious affiliations. It is important that written information encompasses the needs of birth fathers as well as birth mothers, so that they are encouraged to be involved in the process. It should be translated into minority languages if appropriate to the area. The information should highlight the agency's

policies for taking account of children's racial, cultural, religious and linguistic backgrounds in making adoptive placements.

Agreements and adoption

32.   The Act has been amended to make more secure the placement of the child where birth parents have indicated at an earlier stage that they agree to the proposed freeing or adoption application. In addition to the agreement required by the court, there is a new agreement which relates to the actions of the adoption agency. The agency, when it is notifying birth mothers and fathers, whether or not they have relevant rights, or guardians that it considers adoption or freeing to be in the best interests of the child, should also send the memorandum in Schedule 4 (which describes the adoption process) or the memorandum in Schedule 5 (whch describes the freeing for adoption process) as appropriate. Parents or guardians are asked to sign a certificate to say they have received and understood the memorandum. Where a parent or parents have parental responsibilities and rights in relation to the child, or where there is a guardian, they are also asked to complete either the certificate in Schedule 6 which will indicate whether they agree to their child being placed for adoption, or the certificate in Schedule 7 which will indicate whether they agree to the local authority applying to free their child for adoption. The procedures which should be followed, depending on whether or not agreement is forthcoming, are outlined in paragraphs 142-153 below.

Section 27

33.   When an adoption, or freeing for adoption, application is being heard by a court, the court must be satisfied that birth mothers and fathers who have relevant rights or guardians agree freely and unconditionally to an adoption order being made. A reporting officer appointed by the court will be responsible for witnessing such agreements. The court may dispense with the need for agreement in certain circumstances. The grounds for the court dispensing with agreement are that the parent or guardian

Section 16

- is not known, cannot be found or is incapable of giving agreement, or

- is withholding agreement unreasonably, or

- has persistently failed, without reasonable cause, to fulfil one or other of the following parental responsibilities in relation to the child

    (i)   the responsibility to safeguard and promote the child's health, development and welfare, or

    (ii)   if the child is not living with him or her the responsibility to maintain personal relations and direct contact with the child on a regular basis, or

- has seriously ill-treated the child, whose reintegration into the same household as the parent or guardian is, because of the serious ill-treatment or for other reasons, unlikely.

Services for birth parents relinquishing a child

34.   When birth parents are considering having their baby adopted, they should be offered counselling and advice about all the available options to ensure that they have the time and opportunity to make a careful and informed choice. The advice should include the names and addresses of any adoption societies which are available

Regulation 1

in the area which might meet a birth parent's wishes to have his or her child brought up in a particular religious persuasion.

35.   Although, in most situations, the agency will be approached by an unmarried birth mother, she should be encouraged to involve the birth father, wherever possible, in planning for the child unless this would not be in the child's interests. Initially, some birth mothers are reluctant to agree to this, or even to give information about the father, but many agree once they appreciate the importance for the baby's future of having this information. Often birth fathers are willing to share information and to be involved in planning for the baby. This can be valuable for the child in the future.

36.   If the birth mother or birth parents decide that it is in the best interests of their baby to be placed for adoption, they will need support to come to terms with the implications of their decision. The work with the parents will begin to be much more specific in gathering information and discussing the more practical aspects of the adoption process, for example

Schedules 6 & 7 to the Regulations

- the legal process, including the option of pursuing a freeing order with consent under section 18 of the 1978 Act, if this is appropriate. The birth mother and father, if she or he has the relevant legal rights, should be told about the agreement which they will be asked to sign. The contents of the memoranda should be disclosed to them, although they must not be asked to sign the memoranda until after the agency has decided that adoption is in their child's best interests

- issues about possible contact in the future. The various options for this should be explored with the emphasis placed on the welfare of the child.

37.   The social worker should discuss with the birth parents the importance that medical history and information about themselves and their families may have for their child's future. With their agreement, the social worker should obtain as much information as possible and complete an appropriate report, such as BAAF Form A. Given current rapid developments in genetic understanding, all information provided by the parents should be recorded, including ill health or deaths of the wider family, even if its relevance is not immediately apparent. The form should be forwarded to the medical adviser who will advise the adoption panel of the possible implications for the child of the information supplied.

38.   Each agency will have their own process for arranging care for the baby and for selecting prospective adopters but they should ensure that the birth parent is encouraged to be as involved in the process as possible, provided that is in the child's interests.

39.   The period immediately following the birth is a particularly sensitive time and the birth mother should be offered support. Close links should be established with medical staff so that there is a consistent approach to ascertaining the mother's feelings and reactions to the baby. Although the worker will have discussed with the mother her feelings about seeing the baby and the immediate post-natal care of the baby, the depth of feeling following the birth may still surprise the birth mother. Birth mothers who do not see their baby often later regret this. They should, therefore, be encouraged to see the baby in order to come to terms with giving up

the child. It is good practice to have two photographs taken shortly after the birth; one to remain with the baby, and the other to be offered to the birth mother. If she does not want it at that point, she should be made aware that it will be kept in the adoption file and will be available to her if she wants it at a later date.

40.   If, following the birth, the mother changes her mind about the adoption, she should have an opportunity to discuss the implications of this with the social worker and to consider what support she may require to look after the baby. In voluntary agencies, this is likely to require liaison with the relevant local authority.

41.   Agencies may sometimes work with a mother who has concealed her pregnancy up to the time of childbirth. The worker should assist the birth mother to make her own decision and ensure that she has time to do so. She should not be put under undue pressure by other family members who will need time separately to talk about their feelings. This may mean considering a brief placement for the baby in a foster home to give the birth mother time to reach a decision for her and her baby. The health implications for the baby of a concealed pregnancy should be discussed with the agency medical adviser as soon as possible.

42.   In some circumstances, it might be appropriate to consider a placement directly with adoptive parents once the baby is ready to leave hospital. For example, some birth parents and adopters are concerned that the baby should be able to bond with adoptive parents as soon as possible and are worried about the implications of a move to a temporary foster carer as an interim measure. A direct placement might, on occasion, involve the birth parents directly giving the care of the baby to the adopters or even some elements of shared care in the hospital. Such placements should be considered

- where the plan for adoption is made some weeks or months before the birth

- where the parents appear certain about their decision

- if the adopters can cope with any medical complications

- where the agency has prospective adopters who are prepared to deal with the additional uncertainty involved.

43.   In order to facilitate a direct placement a link with prospective adopters should be recommended in principle by the adoption panel before the baby's birth. If the direct placement then goes ahead, the recommendation for the link should be confirmed by the adoption panel. The placement would initially be a fostering placement until the link has been approved by the adoption agency.

44.   Whether the baby is placed directly from the hospital with adoptive parents or following a period in a pre-adoptive foster home, the birth parents should normally be encouraged to become involved in the selection of an adoptive family. Agencies normally have more than one couple available to adopt a baby and they should consider discussing two or three of these who seem appropriate with the birth parents using non-identifying information. If the birth parents express a preference, this may be for a reason which is important to them, and the adoption panel should take this into account.

45.   Occasionally, agencies may be approached by a birth parent of an older child who requests that the child be placed for adoption. Sometimes this will highlight

the need for some other type of service but for a small number of children adoption may be the best outcome. Such parents should be supported and offered appropriate counselling and advice so that they can be helped to identify what is right for both them and their child.

Services for Birth Parents when Children who are Looked After are Placed for Adoption

46.   Where a child is looked after and a return to his or her family no longer seems appropriate, it is important that parents are informed of the likely direction of the agency's planning well before the child care review at which the option of pursuing an adoptive placement is discussed. The parents need the opportunity to express their point of view, including any anger and concerns. Information, counselling and support offered at an early stage may help the parents to focus on the needs of the child and in time come to terms with the agency's decision. Some parents will, however, remain opposed to adoption, or will feel the need to demonstrate to their child that they "fought to keep" him or her.

47.   Once a decision has been made to plan for adoption it can be difficult for the social worker, who will be progressing this plan, to be seen by a parent as supportive if the parent does not agree with that course of action. In such instances, consideration should be given to involving a second social worker to work directly with the parent. If it is not possible to involve a second social worker, then other forms of support should be considered for the parents. Parents should also be urged to seek legal advice and representation.

48.   Parents should be enabled at each stage of the process to state their wishes and feelings about the proposed plan in ways which allow them to feel they have been listened to. They should be assured that their views will be fully presented by the social worker to the adoption panel and that, if the case reaches court, the sheriff will take their views into account and will only make an adoption order or freeing for adoption order if he or she is satisfied that this is in the child's best interests.

49.   There should also be discussion with the birth parents about information which will be given to the adoptive parents and thus, ultimately, to their child. Where possible, they should be encouraged to provide photographs and other mementoes of the child's past. Parents who are in agreement with the agency's plans, or not actively opposing them, may be able to tell their child that they support his or her move to adopters, either in person or in writing.

Continuing support to birth parents

50.   The birth parent should, wherever it is practicable and in the best interests of the child, be given the opportunity prior to the placement to meet with the prospective adoptive parents who are linked with the child. It should be emphasised to both the birth parents and the prospective adopters that this meeting is not to allow the birth parents to vet the adoptive parents but to offer knowledge and, if possible, reassurance about the child's placement.

51.   The emotions involved for the birth parents when their child is being placed for adoption are often profound. Visits to the child just prior to his or her placement

for adoption can be very emotional and it will be hard for birth parents not to show their child the extent of the distress they feel. Preparation for these visits and support after them are essential for the birth parents, the child, and his or her carers.

52.   Occasionally, a birth mother or father who has consented to her or his child being placed for adoption, changes her or his mind and requests that the child be returned to her or his care. In these circumstances, the consent of the court or the agency is needed for the child to be removed from the adoptive placement even before any petition has been lodged. In order to establish whether this is in the child's best interests the agency should consider

Section 27

- the child's legal status

- the views of the child, if he or she is old enough and of sufficient maturity to have a view

- whether grounds exist which would allow dispensation of parental consent at a contested adoption application

- the length and stability of the placement with prospective adopters

- whether there are any concerns about the child's safety or well being if he or she is returned to a parent in which case appropriate steps should be taken

- where applicable, the views of the children's hearing

- whether the circumstances of the birth parents have changed

- the stage reached in the adoption process.

The welfare of the child must be the paramount consideration in making this decision.

53.   If it is decided that the child should be returned to the care of the birth parents this should be done in a way which meets the child's needs and support should be offered to the birth parents and the prospective adoptive parents.

54.   Usually it is several months after a placement that the birth mother and the birth father, if he has the relevant legal rights, are asked by the reporting officer to sign the formal agreement to adoption. This can bring back a lot of the pain, even to those who felt they were coping, and this is a time when the birth parent may need to be offered additional support.

55.   Agencies are required to offer counselling to birth parents if they have a problem about adoption and an increasing number are returning to the agencies which arranged their child's adoption. Some birth parents are seeking an opportunity to discuss unresolved feelings, others may simply be looking for information about their child which often the agency may not have or may not be able to divulge to them. In these circumstances, it is helpful if agencies record up-to-date information about the birth parents on the adoption record so that if the child ever contacts the agency, these details would be available for him or her. Birth parents should be informed about Birthlink, the Adoption Contact Register for Scotland which is maintained by Family Care, in order that they can record their details there. Some birth parents find mutual support groups a useful resource and they should be informed about these where they exist.

Section 1

56.   Some birth parents decide to try to trace their adopted child. If the adopted person is now a mature adult, some agencies are prepared to assist birth parents by

letting either the adopted person or the adoptive family know that the birth parent has been in touch, thus offering them the option of deciding whether they want contact with the birth parent. Such approaches need to be handled carefully, and are not appropriate in all cases.

Other birth family members

57.   Adoption will affect the whole birth family and it may be that other family members need help to deal with the impact that it has on them. It can be helpful, if the birth parents are agreeable, for other family members to be involved in the process of collating the information to be passed on to the adoptive family, and they can also be helpful in building up a picture of the family's medical history.

58.   Sometimes, birth family members approach an agency seeking information about an adopted child or adult. Care must be exercised not to breach confidentiality. It is usually helpful if the birth parent is aware that relatives have approached the agency but this may not always be appropriate or even achievable. For instance, a sibling who was adopted in a different family may approach the agency. Adopted adults are often very interested in tracing siblings and agencies should consider facilitating this contact if it seems appropriate. It can be very helpful in some situations, for example where the birth parent has died, to have information about other interested relatives should the adopted person approach the agency.

Services for Adoptive Parents

Recruitment

59.   There are enough suitable prospective adopters for most healthy babies and very young children. However, finding a suitable family for even slightly older children, children from ethnic minorities, sibling groups, and those with special needs is much harder. In order to heighten public awareness of the needs of these children, agencies should organise regular publicity campaigns using a variety of media. There is room for local, regional and national publicity and recruitment, and agencies may wish to work co-operatively to maximise effective use of resources. Small agencies may find that their demand for adopters, or adopters able to parent particular types of children, fluctuates, and that joint working with other agencies is more likely to produce the adopters they need at the time when they need them.

60.   Some agencies have found particular difficulty in recruiting families from ethnic minority groups. Such families are more likely to apply to adopt if appropriate ways of making contact with them and their organisations, of informing them about adoption and of building confidence in the agency are found. Recruitment of ethnic minority workers can be helpful to this process.

Providing written information

61.   It is important that prospective adopters know the standard of service they can expect as well as what is asked of them during the assessment process. Adoption agencies should ensure that they have available written information about adoption. This should include details of the preparation and home study process, giving likely time scales for completion, together with information about how applicants are accepted to be adoptive parents and then linked with children. It is helpful to include non-identifying information about children needing adoption.

Establishing criteria for applicants

62.   Agencies should make available to any person with an interest a written   *Regulation 10(1)*
statement of the general criteria which they apply for the purpose of considering
whether any person may be accepted for assessment as adoptive parents. Criteria
should be clearly set out so that enquirers can judge easily whether or not they meet
the requirements. If the agency does not accept an application from someone because   *Regulations 10(4)*
he or she does not meet their criteria, they must notify that person in writing.
Where it seems likely that another agency would accept the application, it is helpful
to pass this information to the applicant.

63.   Agencies need to consider their criteria carefully and review them from time   *Regulation 10(2)*
to time.

64.   The matters it may be appropriate to address in general criteria include

- the effects of marital status on the application and any requirements
  concerning the length of the relationship or the marriage

- the age range of the applicants in relation to the age of the children waiting
  for adoption. (Where a waiting list operates, it should be clear whether age
  limits relate to the time when applicants contact the agency, or age at the
  time of approval)

- the health of applicants and how any history of serious illness or disability
  may affect their application

- how criminal convictions will affect their application and any which will
  automatically preclude assessment

- whether current infertility investigations and treatment preclude assessment
  being undertaken

- whether, in the case of adoption societies, there are specifications about
  religious affiliation and observance.

65.   As the range of children requiring adoptive placements has changed and the
complexity of their needs has increased, a much wider range of adoptive applicants
has been needed.

66.   The 1978 Act states that adoptive applicants must have attained the age of
twenty-one (except for a married couple, one of whom is a parent of the child and
has attained the age of eighteen). Applications can be from

- a married couple

- a single person

- a married person who is applying on his or her own because his or her
  spouse cannot be found, or they are permanently separated and living apart
  or, because of ill health, the spouse is incapable of making an application for
  an adoption order.

67.   Many applicants will pursue adoption because they are unable to have a child
of their own. Some may be clear about the reason for their infertility while many
others will not; some will not have had the opportunity of counselling about their
infertility and a referral for counselling may be appropriate. The agency will need

to consider issues of infertility at an early stage with applicants in order to assess whether the couple are ready to consider adoption in a positive way and not merely as a response to their fertility problems.

68.   Undergoing infertility treatment is itself a stressful experience and, where it is ongoing, is likely to be the enquirer's primary focus. In these circumstances, a whole-hearted commitment to adoption may be difficult. The social worker must, therefore, be prepared to spend adequate time talking about these issues with enquirers and try to ensure they make an objective and well-timed decision about the appropriateness of applying to adopt. Even where an agency's general criteria preclude assessment of applicants who are still undergoing fertility treatment, the subsequent timing of an assessment will be important in terms of the applicant's readiness to adopt.

69.   Adopters need to have sufficient health and vigour to bring up a child until adulthood, especially during the demanding years of adolescence. Both age, in comparison to the age of children needing placement, and the health history of applicants will be considerations in establishing general criteria. In addition, where there are too many applicants for a particular group of children, for instance new born healthy babies, stricter criteria may be necessary in order to reduce the number of applicants to a manageable level. It is important, where such criteria are used that people who are not accepted for assessment are not left with the impression that they are unsuitable to be parents.

70.   It should be made clear to applicants that meeting the general criteria does not automatically mean that they will be suitable adopters. The decision to approve someone as an adopter depends upon his or her ability to promote the welfare of a child or children. Where an applicant's attributes or lifestyle are ones that could lead him or her, and a child placed, to experience prejudice from wider society, the agency should seriously consider the effect such prejudice might have on the child. The welfare of the child should be the sole determinant of such a decision.

Responding to enquiries

71.   Information meetings can be an informal way of giving information about adoption, and about the general criteria the agency has for prospective adopters, in a way which does not commit participants to further contact with the agency. It is very helpful if experienced adopters can talk at these meetings about their experiences. Provision should be made, where appropriate, for those whose first language is not English.

72.   An interview with a social worker should be offered to enquirers, either at the point of contact or following an information meeting, to allow them to find out more about adoption, and whether it is appropriate for them. It is important that workers undertaking these interviews are aware of the needs of children who require adoptive placements and of the general criteria which the agency has for prospective adopters. Enquirers should be helped to understand the responsibilities which adoptive parents have in addition to those normally expected of parents.

73.   During the initial interview, the worker should discuss the statutory checks which will be made with enquirers accepted for assessment so that they can identify whether they think, for example, that there are medical problems or recorded criminal convictions which may have a bearing on their application. It may be necessary to

arrange an interpreter for some ethnic minority families to ensure that enquirers fully understand the information on adoption and what would be required from them should they decide to proceed.

Preparation groups

74.   Once they have been accepted for assessment applicants should, wherever possible, be given the opportunity to attend preparation groups which are an important part of the preparation process. Ideally, applicants should attend before the assessment starts but some agencies will not have sufficient numbers of people interested at the same time to ensure this. In rural areas such groups may be difficult to arrange. It may be helpful for some agencies to work co-operatively in order to provide preparation groups or to consider the provision of distance training materials.

75.   Preparation groups should have inputs from social workers and from experienced adopters. Input from a medical adviser can also be helpful. Groups should help applicants to decide whether adoption is right for them and increase their knowledge and understanding of the issues involved in parenting someone else's child. They should provide information about possible contact in adoption, on talking to the child about adoption and about the legal and medical aspects of adoption. They should look at the effects on children of separation and loss, and of physical and sexual abuse and neglect.

The assessment

76.   For those accepted for assessment, the process should be an educative as well as an evaluative one which should contribute to the applicants' decision as to whether adoption is right for them. It should help to prepare them for the reality of looking after a child who has been separated from his or her birth parents and to identify their own strengths and aspects of a placement about which they feel less confident. Its statutory function is, however, an evaluation by the agency of an applicant's suitability to be an adoptive parent. Whilst considerable emphasis may be placed on self-assessment, it should be made clear to applicants that their approval as adopters will be solely the decision of the agency.

77.   Applicants should be asked to complete an application form which, if they *Regulation 10(3)* are successful against the general criteria, will trigger the assessment process. If there is to be a delay before the assessment can begin applicants should be informed of the likely length of the delay and the reasons for it. The application form should be based on Part IV Schedule 2 of the Adoption Agencies Regulations. Applicants should be informed that police records will be consulted to check for previous convictions. The police should also be asked to check the records of all other adult members of the household with the members' permission. Authorities should note that the Rehabilitation of Offenders Act 1974 Exceptions Orders apply to these checks. A record of convictions should be discussed with the applicant and will, dependent on their nature, not necessarily preclude approval but will require careful consideration and consultation with senior staff and the adoption panel. Authorities should check their own current and previous records in respect of the applicants and other members of the household. Where the prospective adopters live in the area of another authority that authority's views must be sought. Where there has been a previous application to foster or adopt, the relevant agency should be consulted. Applicants should be asked to provide the names and addresses of two

personal referees who are not close relatives. They should also be informed that they will be required to have a full medical assessment.

Regulation 9(1)   78.   The medical report should be obtained no more than twelve months before the application is considered by the adoption panel. It is good practice if medical and police checks are updated prior to any linking with a child if more than twelve months have elapsed since the decision that the applicants were suitable to adopt.

79.   In some instances, applicants will decide to withdraw during the process. Since part of the preparation is about enabling applicants to make an informed choice, withdrawal should be accepted positively. On other occasions it will become obvious during the approval process that an applicant is unlikely to be suitable for some reason. The social worker's concerns should be discussed with his or her managers and on occasions this may lead to the adoption panel being approached for guidance. Sometimes, when the social worker discusses such concerns with the applicant he or she will not accept the concerns and will wish to continue with the application. The social worker should present such situations to the adoption panel who will make a recommendation as to whether the assessment should continue or not. Agencies should consider giving applicants the right to ask for reconsideration in situations where it is decided not to continue with an assessment. (See paragraphs 123-124 below).

80.   All home studies of prospective adopters should be carried out by qualified social workers who have, where necessary, access to staff with particular knowledge about child placement for advice and guidance. Home studies should normally be completed no more than six months from the application being received.

81.   Some issues to be considered in the home study are contained in Annex 1 to this chapter.

82.   The referees referred to paragraph 77 should be people who know the applicants well personally, rather than professionally in the way a doctor or minister might do. The social worker should normally interview the referees and the confidential status of the reference should be made clear. If a referee lives at a distance which makes it impossible for him or her to be visited by the social worker, arrangements should be made to have the referee interviewed by someone from the local social work department or social services departments in the area in which the referee lives.

83.   A full medical assessment should be carried out on applicants by their GP and a written report, such as BAAF Form Adult 1, completed. This gives information on the applicant's medical history and that of their family together with details of the applicant's current physical and mental health. These details should be forwarded to the agency medical adviser who will arrange for any further information to be obtained. In the case of other adults resident in the house, it is not necessary for them to be medically examined but, with their agreement, their GP should be contacted for information.

84.   Applicants who are applying for a second child or to adopt a child they are already fostering need to go through the process of the home study and the formal checks again although the focus of the home study will be different. For second

time adopters the issues addressed may include the steps they have taken to talk to their child about adoption, how they have adjusted to being parents, and, if there are any arrangements for contact with the birth parents, how these have worked. For foster carers adopting a child already living with them the issues addressed may include how and why they have reached the decision to adopt, the child's views, how they and the child will adapt to a different status and probably a different level of support, any contact issues and any financial considerations.

85.   Some applicants may find it hard to understand why some of the information is required. In particular, this may be the case if the applicants come from a culture where alternative family arrangements are made more informally. The information requirement should not be compromised but careful explanation should be given as to why it is required and possibly some adaptation made as to how it is acquired.

86.   It is important that ethnic minority families feel that workers respect their racial identity, their culture, language and religion, and have some understanding of these. If possible, an ethnic minority worker should be involved in the preparation process, especially in the initial stages when applicants will be most anxious. The home study should be set within the context of the culture of the applicants and where necessary, informed advice should be sought by the social worker. In some circumstances, it may be necessary to use an interpreter who should be helped to become familiar with adoption work.

87.   Any children of the applicant should be as fully involved as possible within the limits of their age and understanding. The social worker should spend time with the children using a variety of techniques to explain what is proposed and find out how they feel about it. Advice and materials might also be provided to applicants so that they can undertake preparation of their children. The reaction of the applicant's own children can be crucial to the success or failure of a placement.

88.   Social workers undertaking home studies should be aware of research findings which indicate the kind of families and kinds of children who do best together. For example, placements of children who are close in age to an adopter's own children have a higher disruption rate; and siblings tend to settle better if placed together rather than separately.

Post approval support

89.   Following the applicant's acceptance as an adoptive parent, the social worker should continue to visit on a regular basis. The focus of these contacts should be to continue to discuss with the applicants the resource they are offering, to consider with them any possible links with a child, and for them to share information about any changes in personal circumstances.

90.   If possible, a lengthy wait for a placement after applicants have been accepted by an agency should be avoided. As time passes, it may be hard for them to maintain their initial enthusiasm and commitment. Nevertheless, prospective adopters need time to prepare themselves practically and psychologically for a placement and, except where the child is already fostered in the placement or they are being approved for a specific child, it is not usually appropriate that recommendations that adopters are approved and then linked with a child are made at the same adoption panel meeting.

91.   If the agency has no children available who link with what the adopters can offer they should consider with the adopters the possibility of a referral to a resource exchange, such as BAAF Link, within a reasonable time scale. For some applicants who are offering a very specific resource, eg for a Down's Syndrome child, such a referral might be initiated at the time of approval, unless the agency has a suitable child.

92.   Approval should not normally last for an indefinite period. If a placement has not been made within a specified period, for instance for two years, the adoption panel should review whether the circumstances of the prospective adopters have changed and consider whether the terms of their approval need to be confirmed or altered.

The Adoption Panel

Statutory functions of the panel

Regulation 7   93.   An adoption agency is required to have an adoption panel except where the adoption agency is not carrying out the functions specified in regulation 11. Large agencies may have more than one panel.

94.   Local authorities will also have a fostering panel established under the Fostering of Children (Scotland) Regulations 1996, which may have the same membership as the adoption panel. However, the two are different bodies and their proceedings must be minuted separately.

95.   The functions of the adoption panel are

Regulation 11
- to consider whether adoption is in the best interests of a particular child and, if so, whether a freeing application should be made under section 18 of the 1978 Act

- to provide a written report of the consideration given by them to alternatives to adoption and in circumstances where adoption with parental contact is recommended, why adoption is recommended rather than an alternative course of action

- to consider whether a prospective adopter is suitable to be an adoptive parent. This will generally follow the completion of a home study, but it may be earlier if the worker identifies issues which he or she considers may lead to the applicant being deemed unsuitable

- to consider whether a prospective adopter would be a suitable adoptive parent for a particular child. A recommendation cannot be made about prospective adopters being suitable for a particular child unless a recommendation has also been made that adoption is in the best interests of the child.

Where the child is linked to a prospective adopter from another agency, the linking must be considered by the adoption panel of the agency with responsibility for the child.

Supplementary functions of the panel

Regulation 11(6)   96.   The Regulations give agencies discretion to seek the Panel's advice on other relevant matters. Such matters might be

- to consider permanency plans for children

- to consider plans to place siblings together or separately

- to monitor and review the implementation of plans for children. The Panel could be given the duty of reviewing cases where children have been freed for adoption and are not placed within six months of the order being made. This duty must be repeated every six months until a placement is made or the order is revoked

- to review after a specified time approved adoptive parents who have not been linked with a child

- to consider reports on the disruption of any adoptive placement and make recommendations about whether adoption is still in the best interests of the child, and whether the prospective adopters should still be approved and, if so, the terms of their approval

- to consider matters relating to financial assistance for adopters, for example approved adoption allowances or the payment of legal expenses incurred by the adopters in obtaining an adoption order.

Regulation 21

Membership of the panel

97.   The Regulations specify a minimum of six members but, in practice, agencies tend to have more. The agency should determine the appropriate number for their particular circumstances.

Regulation 7(4)

98.   Apart from the medical adviser and the legal adviser, the Regulations do not specify the composition of the Panel, only requiring that the numbers, qualifications and experience of members enable it to discharge its functions effectively and that each member is competent to assess whether any recommendations in relation to children are likely to promote their welfare throughout their lives.

Regulation 6

99.   Men and women must both be represented on the Panel. Panels should seek to reflect a range of knowledge and experience, particularly in relation to adoption and to children separated from their families, and their composition should enable different perspectives on these issues to be obtained. Parenting experience, particularly as an adoptive parent, will be important. Confidentiality should be stressed and consideration might be given to panel members giving a signed undertaking on this matter.

Regulation 7

100.   A balance should also be achieved between representatives from agency staff, management committee members or elected representatives of the agency, and representatives from the communities served by the agency. Membership should, where possible, reflect the racial and cultural heritage of the children and adopters being considered. Where this cannot be achieved, co-option for a particular panel meeting, where a child or family from a minority group is being discussed, should be considered.

Terms of appointment

101.   Agencies should have clearly stated policies on the terms and duration of appointments to the Panel, the duties (including the duty of confidentiality) and expected time commitment of membership, any expenses that can be paid and the

procedure for reviewing membership. With the exception of the medical and legal advisers, appointments should normally be for a fixed term (with renewal of membership an option) but should ensure continuity and consistency of expertise.

The role of the chairperson

102.   Although not required by Regulations a chairperson should be appointed by a senior officer of a local authority or the chairperson of the Management Committee in the case of a voluntary agency.

103.   For local authorities, there are advantages in the chairperson being an agency manager or elected representative with child care experience but, if at all possible, not one who is the immediate line manager for this area of work. They should have a thorough understanding of the structure and policies of the agency and be aware of the financial and organisational procedures in respect of adoption. In smaller authorities or voluntary agencies, the chairperson may be a member of the agency's management committee, or an independent person who is familiar with the workings of the agency, and who has experience and interest in the child care field.

104.   The chairperson does not have to be present for the Panel to be quorate, but a depute chairperson should also be appointed by the agency who can chair the Panel in the absence of the chairperson.

The role of the legal adviser

Regulation 6 105.   The adoption agency has a duty to appoint such solicitors, or advocates as it considers necessary for the purpose of providing it with legal advice. The legal adviser's advice at the Panel will enable members to explore the legal issues in each case and to clarify the alternatives to adoption. The legal adviser must be present or give written advice when the Panel is considering whether adoption is in the best interests of a child, and whether or not an application for a freeing order should be pursued. The legal adviser cannot make up the quorum.

The role of the medical adviser

Regulation 6 106.   The agency must appoint a registered medical practitioner, or practitioners, as a medical adviser. The medical adviser will interpret medical information for the Panel and advise on its relevance for a child's placement for adoption or on prospective adopters' suitability to adopt a child. The medical adviser will also advise the Panel of the eligibility of a child on health grounds, for an adoption allowance. The wider role of the medical adviser outside the adoption panel is described in paragraphs 126-137 below.

107.   Agencies will need to consider whether the medical adviser has purely an advisory role to the Panel or whether he or she is a full voting member of the Panel. Medical advisers usually build up a great deal of expertise in adoption issues and full membership can be helpful. However, the medical adviser cannot make up the quorum.

Information required by the panel

Regulations 8 & 9 108.   If a child is being presented to the Panel to consider whether adoption is in his or her best interests the Panel require

- a detailed case history and description of the child in a specified format (for example, BAAF Form E) which will include all the particulars in Part 1 Schedule 2 to the Regulations. The report should include an outline of the alternatives to adoption which have been considered and why it is considered that the alternatives will not meet the child's needs as well as adoption. If it is intended that contact with one or both birth parents will continue after adoption, the report should outline why adoption is recommended rather than an alternative course of action

- any reports prepared giving legal advice in relation to adoption.

In addition, the following may be helpful to the Panel

- in the case of a child who is looked after by the local authority, the minute of the child care review which recommended that adoption should be considered

- any planning or other relevant reports, eg psychiatric, psychological or school reports.

109.   The medical adviser will offer advice to the Panel based on the medical report which has been completed on the child (such as BAAF Forms C or D) which should have been completed within the previous twelve months, together with any updates which he or she has requested. Written information about the child's birth parents and about the birth (such as in BAAF Forms B1, B2 or B3) should accompany the medical form.

Regulations 8 & 9

110.   If prospective adopters are being presented to the Panel, the Panel should have

- the home study report

- a brief report on any second opinion visit or interview carried out if this is separate from the home study report.

The medical adviser should have the medical reports on the applicants.

111.   If a link between a child and adopters is proposed the Panel is likely to require

- information on the child as outlined above

- any other relevant reports on the child, particularly if he or she has waited a considerable time for a link with an adoptive family

- the minute of the Panel which endorsed the plan for adoption for the child

- information on the adopters as outlined above

- the minute of the Panel which recommended approval of the prospective adopters

- a linking form or the minute of any linking meeting

- a report on the post-placement and post-adoption support which will be provided for the child and adopters.

112.   Information should be circulated sufficiently prior to the date of the Panel to allow panel members adequate reading time. The confidentiality of the

information and the arrangements for sending it and storing it, should be detailed in the agency's procedures. Papers should normally be collected or posted by recorded delivery and collected in at the end of meetings of the Panel.

The views of the child

Section 6   113.   Panel members must take into account the views of the child about any plan for his or her future when making a recommendation. Generally, the child's views will be represented by the social worker and the carer, but it may also be appropriate to offer the child the opportunity to write something about himself or herself and about the plans for his or her future which can be attached to the information being presented. Children aged twelve or over will be required to agree to adoption so consideration of their views is essential. There may occasionally be circumstances when it is appropriate for an older child to attend part of the adoption panel so that he or she can represent his or her own views and can feel a full part of the decision making process. This should only happen where the Panel has had the opportunity to consider the merits of such attendance in advance.

Attendance at the panel and presentation of cases

114.   In presenting reports on children or families to the adoption panel, the key staff member is the social worker who has undertaken the assessment. It is desirable that his or her line manager, should also be present to support the worker and to offer his or her opinion about the applicants. When reports on children are being presented it is helpful if the current carer can be present.

115.   Agencies must invite prospective adopters to attend the adoption panel which is considering their suitability as adopters. It will give panel members the chance to raise issues directly with the applicants and also allows the applicants the opportunity to meet, discuss with and give their own views to the people who will be making the recommendation about their application. Panels will need to decide whether they wish to invite applicants for the whole discussion of their application or whether they will only be invited to parts of the discussion. Panel members and particularly the chairperson should be able to deal with any anxieties which applicants may have about attending the adoption panel and be able to put them at their ease. Some applicants may still, nevertheless, find attendance too daunting and non-attendance should not be seen as signifying a lack of commitment to adoption.

116.   If a link between a child and a family is being considered by the Panel, it is good practice for the social worker for the child and the social worker for the family to be present. It may be helpful for the child's current carers also to be present for the discussion on the child, but because of issues of confidentiality, he or she should leave while the potential adopters are being discussed.

117.   On occasions the Panel may wish to invite someone to provide specialist knowledge and advice e.g. to give advice about the beliefs of a particular religious group. Care must be taken to ensure the confidentiality of the case being discussed.

118.   Agencies will vary in the way they expect cases to be presented to the Panel. Whatever format is used, it should enable full and focused discussion and all panel members should have an opportunity to air questions and concerns. If the Panel *Regulation 11(5)(6)*   feel there are significant gaps in information, they should ask the social worker to

seek further information or clarification and defer the recommendation until a subsequent panel meeting.

Advice giving

119. As recognised in paragraph 96, some agencies use their adoption panel to consider and advise more generally about issues which arise in adoption work. For instance the work to prepare children for adoption, issues about sibling placements or contact, concerns about applicants which have arisen during the approval process or post placement, or post adoption situations where there are problems. The different perspectives of the panel members can be used to good effect in such situations and it gives the worker access to a body with considerable expertise in adoption matters. Panel members need to be clear that, in the circumstances, they are not sitting as a recommendation making meeting but rather as an advisory group with adoption expertise. Such consultations should be placed separately on the agenda from the main matters of the meeting.

The decision-making Process

120. The agency should set up a clear, simple and efficient process for considering the adoption panel's recommendations and deciding on the appropriate course of action. Agencies should appoint a nominated decision-maker. The agency is obliged to make a decision within fourteen days of the Panel recommendation and if its decision is contrary to the Panel's recommendation, it must record its reasons in writing. It must notify the parents and prospective adopters of the decision within a further seven days. Consideration should be given as to how children are notified.

Regulation 12

121. It is important that the agency decision-maker is independent of the Panel. He or she should be a senior member of staff, or in voluntary agencies may be the chairperson of the Management Committee, and should be knowledgeable about adoption matters. Where the agency decision-maker attends the Panel he or she should not seek to influence its recommendations. Another decision-maker should be available for times when the decision-maker is on leave or off sick.

122. The minute of the adoption panel is an important record of the meeting which should assist the agency to reach decisions and ensure they are carried out appropriately. It should, therefore, be a full minute which reflects the discussion and the issues which arose leading to how the recommendation was made. A copy of the minute should be kept in the prospective adopter's file and in the child's file.

Representations, complaints and reconsiderations

123. Under the Social Work (Scotland) Act 1968 and the Social Work (Representations Procedure) (Scotland) Directions 1996, children, their parents and adopters have the right to make representations (including complaints) concerning a local authority's discharge or failure to discharge any of their legal functions. In the case of adoption societies, this right is contained in Regulation 4.

124. Given the significance of decisions that an adoption agency makes, agencies may find it helpful to establish a reconsideration procedure for adoptive applicants. This would allow the applicants to ask for a decision made by the adoption agency

in relation to a recommendation from the adoption panel to be reconsidered. The reconsideration procedure, if it is to have credibility, should allow reconsideration independent of the Panel which made the original recommendation. In a large agency this could be a second adoption panel. Children, parents and adoptive applicants should receive written information about the representations and complaints procedure, and adoptive applicants should be given information about the reconsideration procedure if one is established.

Induction and training

125.   Agencies should have procedures for inducting new panel members including the provision of written information, copies of the 1978 Act, Regulations and Guidance and an opportunity to attend the Panel as an observer. Panel members should attend seminars and training courses including those provided by the agency. Relevant training might include issues beyond those directly focused on adoption, such as child protection and separation and loss. The agency should organise appropriate training on a regular basis, both for the Panel as a whole and for individual members such as the medical or legal adviser if they have specific training needs.

The Role of the Medical Adviser
The medical implications of adoption

126.   As the nature of adoption has changed the role of the medical adviser has increased. Some children placed for adoption have special needs as a result of abuse or neglect or because of physical or learning disabilities. There may be significant hereditary conditions in the birth family which could have implications for the child's future health and welfare and for that of their own offspring. Agencies need advice on the implications of such medical issues for placement and adoptive parents need expert help in understanding what these might mean for their child and in securing appropriate services. The agency medical adviser has a unique role to play in this process and can also act as an advocate for the child in securing any health services needed. The responsibilities of the medical adviser also extend to the prospective adopters and the counselling and support which he or she can offer to them both before and after placement can be of great importance.

The legislative framework

Regulations 6 & 7   127.   Adoption agencies are required to appoint one or more doctors as medical advisers to the agency. Where an agency appoints more than one medical adviser, it is helpful if one acts as the co-ordinator of the medical work of the agency. The medical adviser must be appointed as a member of the adoption panel. Their role on the Panel is considered in paragraphs 106-107 of this document.

128.   The Regulations require the medical adviser's involvement in a number of aspects of the agency's decision on individual cases

Schedule 2
- the medical adviser is required to consider and advise on any aspects of the health of the child, his or her birth family and the prospective adopters. The health of the child and the prospective adopters requires to be detailed in a report from a fully registered medical practitioner and this report should have been completed within the previous twelve months

- the medical adviser should consider whether any medical investigations and tests are necessary for the child

Regulation 9(2)

- the medical adviser is required to decide whether a child has a problem of such medical significance as to warrant notice being given, before the child's placement for adoption, to the education authority or the health authority of any special needs for education or medical care. The adoption agency is required to make the notification.

Regulation 19(2)

The agency and its medical adviser should not necessarily confine themselves to the above matters and should identify any medical issues which require investigation and consideration either generally or in individual cases. Where a child is placed with a family approved by another agency, both agencies will need to agree which medical adviser retains responsibility for providing medical advice for the placement. Where the child is to be placed outside his or her current Health Board area, it is usually helpful if the medical adviser is the one for the family's agency as he or she will have links with local medical services.

Evaluation of the health of birth families

129.   As much information as possible about the health of birth parents and the wider family, including genetic information, should be collected by the social worker for the child and this should be shared with the medical adviser prior to the child's medical examination. Further information about the health of birth parents may be provided by the relevant general practitioner with the signed consent of the birth parents. In some circumstances it may not be possible to collect the relevant information. For example, there may be hostility to an adoption placement and a reluctance to co-operate with the agency, or the identity of a birth parent may not be known. However, the social worker and the medical adviser should strive to obtain as much information as possible.

Evaluation of the health of the child

130.   Children to be placed for adoption require a comprehensive medical assessment and examination covering physical, developmental and emotional issues. The findings should be recorded on an appropriate form such as BAAF Forms C, D or YP. The medical assessment and examination should be undertaken by a senior doctor skilled in child health. The medical adviser will also need to gather information from various sources including the general practitioner, the health visitor, the school health service and any specialised services involved with the child.

Regulation 9(1)

131.   Although regulations state that the medical examination should take place within the previous twelve months, this will be too long an interval in many circumstances, for example, with babies and young children where developmental progress is normally rapid. Updates to information should be obtained at the discretion of the medical adviser.

132.   Physical, developmental and emotional problems may be evident prior to the pre-adoption assessment and examination, or may be revealed during the procedure, requiring referral to other health professionals. In some instances a psychological or psychiatric assessment may be needed. The medical adviser should ensure that any recommended examinations, screening procedures or tests on the

child are carried out and that all necessary medical care and support is arranged. The need for ongoing medical assessment or treatment may influence the timing of the placement of the child.

Evaluation of the health of prospective adopters

Regulation 9(2)   133.   Prospective adopters are required to undergo a medical examination undertaken by their general practitioner who will provide a report using appropriate medical forms, such as BAAF Adult 1. It is helpful if the medical examinations and reports can be requested at an early stage in the home study, especially if the applicants have indicated that there may be significant medical issues. This report should be updated annually prior to a placement being made and in certain circumstances the medical adviser may wish to obtain information more regularly.

Medical needs prior to and during placement

134.   The medical adviser has a role in identifying the post-placement medical needs of children placed for adoption and in assisting the agency to fulfil these. The medical adviser should be available for consultation and advice as required during the placement.

Regulation 19(2)   135.   The following should be notified about the child's health

- the prospective adopter's registered general practitioner before the proposed placement together with particulars of the proposed placement. The information should comprise a written report on the child's health history and current state of health

- the Health Board area in which the prospective adopter resides. This should be before the placement commences, if the medical adviser considers the child to have a problem of medical significance to his or her future care

- the education authority if the medical adviser considers the child to have a problem of medical significance or special educational needs.

136.   The statutory involvement of the medical adviser ceases when the adoption order is granted and any further involvement is at the discretion of the adoptive parents and will depend on any service agreement between the NHS Trust and the adoption agency. Where children require continuing specialist medical help, access to the medical adviser can be important and his or her knowledge of the child and adoptive parents may be very helpful.

137.   If a child develops a condition at any stage in the placement which has genetic implications for the birth family, the medical adviser has a role in advising on appropriate action, although it is recognised that it may not be possible to pass information on. Equally, if important additional information about the health of the birth family becomes available after the adoption order is granted, the medical adviser should evaluate the significance of this information and, with the agency, consider how to pass this information to the adoptive family, or to the adopted adult, in an appropriate and sensitive way, giving due consideration to matters of confidentiality.

Notifications and Information to be Provided to Parents, Adopters, the Children's Hearing and other Agencies

Notifications to adopters

138.   Adoptive applicants must be notified in writing if

- it is decided not to accept them for assessment. It will be helpful if reasons are given   *Regulation 10(4)*

- their case has been referred to the adoption panel. Their notification should include a copy of the home study report which will be presented to the panel, excluding any third party information provided in confidence.

The home study should be sent by recorded delivery. Very occasionally, copies of home studies are used inappropriately by prospective adopters. It will help to prevent this happening if it is clear whether any recommendation in the home study for approval is for domestic adoption or overseas adoption.

139.   Once the agency has reached a decision, based on the recommendation of the adoption panel, the agency must within seven days of the decision notify prospective adopters

- whether it considers them to be suitable to be adoptive parents. Again the letter should state that they are considered suitable to be domestic adopters. In the case of overseas adopters, the letter should state that the agency are of the opinion that the applicants would be suitable adopters for a child from abroad. The letter should make it clear that the decision as to whether a child may be brought into this country is a matter for the Home Office immigration department who take the advice of the Social Work Services Group   *Regulation 12(3)*

- if there has been a proposed match with a child, whether they are considered suitable for that particular child.

140.   When a child and prospective adopter have been matched, the adoption agency must provide the prospective adopter with   *Regulation 19(1)*

- written information about the child's background, parentage, health, and mental and emotional development. It is important that information about the child's background includes as much information as is known about the health of the birth family

- written advice about the need to tell the child about his or her adoption and origins, the right of adopted people to obtain information from the Register of Births relating to their adoption and the availability of counselling services

- a report based on the medical findings about the child.

141.   Whilst not required under Regulations, some adoption agencies also supply the adopters with a letter, written to the child, explaining the reasons he or she has been placed for adoption. The adopter is asked to share this with the child as he or she gets older to help the child understand and accept his or her origins and the reasons he or she was placed for adoption.

Notifications to birth parents

142.   Birth parents who have parental responsibilities or a guardian, must be notified, within seven days of the agency decision being made, that the agency has   *Regulation 12(3)*

decided that adoption is in their child's best interests. Where a parent does not have parental responsibilities, the agency should notify him or her if they consider this to be in the child's interests.

Regulation 14(1)   143.   When notifying the parents or a guardian of a decision that adoption is in the child's interests, the adoption agency must send them one of the memoranda in Schedule 4 or 5 of the Regulations (depending on whether the decision is to pursue freeing or adoption). This contains information about the legal process and a certificate stating that they have received, read and understood the memorandum. At the same time, the adoption agency should give the birth parents or guardian a certificate (Schedule 6 or 7) asking them to state whether or not they agree with the plan to place their child for adoption or to apply to free their child for adoption. The adoption agency has a duty to take such steps as are reasonably practicable to make sure that birth parents get the memoranda, sign the certificates and return them to the agency. The requirement to send a memorandum (Schedule 4 or 5) also applies to a parent who does not have parental responsibilities if the agency considers it would be in the child's interests for him or her to receive the notifications. The agency should also ascertain, as far as possible, whether or not such a parent intends to apply for any parental responsibilities or rights in relation to the child.

Regulation 15(1)   144.   If the birth parent returns the certificate indicating he or she consents to the plan, the agency will proceed on the basis that consent to the making of the subsequent adoption or freeing application is likely to be forthcoming. Should the *Regulation 15(3)*   birth parent give consent to the plan, but then subsequently withdraw it, the case should be treated as though consent had not been given, except that, if the child has already been placed for adoption, the child may not be returned to the parent without the permission of the adoption agency or the court.

145.   When a parent of a child who is not the subject of a supervision requirement states that they do not agree to their child being placed for adoption, or it is deemed after twenty-eight days that agreement is unlikely to be forthcoming, an adoption agency which is a local authority must lodge a freeing petition within a further twenty-eight days, unless an adoption application is made within the twenty-eight day period. Where the child is subject to a supervision requirement, the provision in paragraphs 150 and 151 apply. Where originally it was intended to place the child for adoption, but a freeing application now has to be made, the parents should be supplied with information concerning freeing for adoption based on Schedule 5.

Regulation 19(2)   146.   When a child is placed with adoptive parents, the birth parents of the child, including the father of a child who is not and has not been married to the mother where the agency considers this to be in the child's interests, or the guardian, must be notified in writing that the child has been placed for adoption. Where such a child has been placed for adoption and the parent has made a declaration that he or she wishes no further involvement with the child, a notification should not be made unless the parent subsequently withdraws the declaration.

Section 19   147.   If a freeing order is granted, a local authority adoption agency still has certain duties to the birth parents. The local authority has to tell the birth parent whether or not an adoption order has been granted, except where the parent has made a declaration that he or she prefers not to be further involved in any questions concerning his or her child. It can do this at the time the order is made but must do so within fourteen days of the expiry of a twelve month period after the freeing order is made. If on the other hand the child has not been adopted at that stage, there is a duty to tell the birth parent whether or not the child has been placed in an adoptive home. If the child is placed for adoption or adopted subsequently, the local authority has a duty to tell the birth parent when that happens. The birth parent must be informed if the adoption placement disrupts.

148.   If, after twelve months, the child has not been placed for adoption or been adopted, the parent may apply for a revocation of the freeing order. While the application is pending, the local authority cannot place the child in an adoptive home without leave of the court. If the parent's application is successful, the court will decide on whom to award the parental responsibilities and rights for the child.

Section 20

149.   The adoption agency may apply at any time for a revocation of a freeing order provided an adoption order has not been made and the child is not placed for adoption. The circumstances where the adoption agency would make such an application might be where it has proved impossible to find an adoptive home for the child or an adoptive placement has been disrupted and the adoption panel recommends that adoption is no longer in the child's best interests.

Section 20(1A)

Notifications to a children's hearing

150.   If the child is subject to a supervision requirement and the agency which is a local authority has, after a recommendation has been made by the adoption panel, decided to pursue adoption or a freeing order, it must notify the Principal Reporter of this. Where a voluntary agency has received written agreement to the adoption plan, it should notify the Principal Reporter under section 22(A). Where the local authority adoption agency determines that the parents are unlikely to agree to the proposed adoption or freeing order it must notify the Principal Reporter within seven days of determining that such agreement is unlikely and the Principal Reporter must arrange a hearing to sit within a further twenty-one days.

Regulations 13 and 18

151.   The children's hearing must consider all plans for adoption and freeing, where a child is subject to a supervision requirement and give advice to the court. This means they are able to say whether they think the plan is appropriate or not. If they take the view that the plan is not appropriate the adoption agency is not prevented from going ahead with its plans but it must do so within tight time scales. The local authority must reconsider its plan within twenty-eight days, and decide either to continue with its plan, or not. In reconsidering, it must take into account the advice from the children's hearing and may seek the views of the adoption panel. If it decides to proceed with its plan then it must lodge a freeing application within twenty-eight days from the date of the children's hearing unless the adoption application has already been made. Regardless of the decision reached, the agency must inform the Principal Reporter of its decision. Where a children's hearing agrees with the plan, the accelerated timescales will still apply from the date of the children's hearing decision in cases where birth parents have already indicated that they do not agree.

Regulation 18

Summary of regulations containing provisions for accelerated time scales

152.   There are accelerated time scale duties on adoption agencies in the following adoption or freeing for adoption cases

- any case where the birth parent fails to agree to the proposed adoption or freeing application

- any case where the children's hearing do not agree with the plan (this applies only where the child is subject to a supervision requirement).

In all these cases, a freeing petition is expected to be lodged rapidly unless, as may happen sometimes, the child is already placed with the proposed adoptive parents and they have lodged a petition for adoption within the time limits.

153.   The provisions are laid out in diagrammatic form in Annexes 2 and 3.

Notifications to other agencies

Regulation 19(2)   154.   When a child is placed for adoption the following agencies, in whose area the prospective adopters live, must be notified in writing

- the local authority, giving particulars of the placement

- where the child is of compulsory school age, the education authority, giving particulars of the placement. The notification must take place before the placement if the agency's medical adviser considers the child to have a problem of medical significance or special educational needs

- the Health Board giving particulars of the placement. The notification must take place before the placement if the agency's medical adviser considers the child to have a problem of medical significance to his or her future care.

The local authority must also send a written report of the child's health history and current state of health to the prospective adopters' registered medical practitioner prior to the placement, together with particulars of the proposed placement.

Adoption Allowances
The Adoption Allowance (Scotland) Regulations 1996

155.   The Adoption Allowance (Scotland) Regulations 1996 (subsequently referred to as the 1996 Regulations in this section of the Guidance; references in the margin in this part of the chapter are to those Regulations) replace adoption agency schemes for the payment of adoption allowances under section 51(5) of the 1978 Act. From 1 April 1998, previous adoption allowance schemes will be revoked and all new adoption allowances will be paid in accordance with the 1996 Regulations. Transitional arrangements will be introduced to allow adopters currently in receipt of an allowance to continue to receive payments under the old arrangements. It will no longer be necessary for local authorities to submit adoption allowance schemes to the Secretary of State for approval or amendment. The 1996 Regulations will enable any adoption agency (whether a local authority or an approved society) to pay an adoption allowance within the parameters set by the Regulations which will require them to consider eligibility and assess payment. Adoption allowances should be the exception rather than the norm. However, like the schemes which they replace, the Regulations are intended to give adoption agencies sufficient flexibility to respond to individual needs and circumstances within this overall objective. Research demonstrates the importance of adoption allowances in facilitating the adoption of a number of children who would not otherwise be placed for adoption.

156.   Local authorities are required to maintain an adoption allowance scheme. An approved adoption society, unless it is an agency which normally pays allowances, is under no obligation to maintain a scheme but it is not prevented from paying an allowance in an exceptional case. In such an instance it will need to follow the 1996 Regulations.

157.   The 1996 Regulations reflect the principles which led to the introduction of adoption allowance schemes in 1982. The central principle is still that an adoption allowance can be paid where this will help secure an adoptive home for a child who otherwise could not be readily adopted.

158.   Agencies should note that the term allowance is intended to apply to a periodic or regular payment payable at intervals to be determined by the agency. Where a single lump sum or capital payment is required in connection with the child's circumstances - for example, in order to purchase equipment or to make adaptations to the home - local authorities can assist by exercising other powers and are under an obligation to provide their adoption services in conjunction with their other statutory functions. This applies whether or not an allowance is to be paid. Such legislation includes the Chronically Sick and Disabled Persons Act 1970 and powers which are available in the Children (Scotland) Act 1995 in relation to children in need.

Section 1(3)

Circumstances in which an allowance may be paid

159.   Adoption agencies must consider whether an allowance may be paid for any child whose adoption they are arranging or have arranged, before an adoption order is made. The circumstances under which an allowance may be paid are

Regulation 5(1) of the 1996 Regulations

(a)   the adoption agency is satisfied that the child has established a strong and important relationship with the adopters before the order is made. This will mainly apply where a child has been living with foster carers who wish to adopt him or her but cannot afford to lose their fostering allowance. The foster carers' financial circumstances need to be assessed in the same way as other adopters as they do not have an automatic right to an adoption allowance. It is important that everyone concerned with the placement, including the child, distinguishes that the placement has changed to an adoptive placement. The date of this change should be notified to the prospective adopters in writing and it is helpful if adoption allowance payments commence on that date.

Regulation 3(2)(a) of the 1996 Regulations

(b)   it is desirable that the child be placed with the same adopters as his or her brothers and sisters or with a child with whom he or she has previously shared a home.

Regulation 3(2)(b) of the 1996 Regulations

(c)   at the time of placement for adoption the child is mentally or physically disabled or suffering from emotional or behavioural difficulties and needs special care which requires additional expenditure. The expression mentally or physically disabled is not defined. Children who show emotional or behavioural difficulties may include those who have experienced physical or sexual abuse or both. The medical adviser to the adoption panel will be of special value in evaluating the degree of the child's condition and in providing advice to the agency. Payment of the allowance is intended where the child's condition is serious and long-term. The condition may, for example, lead to a child requiring a special diet, or inflicting heavy wear

Regulation 3(2)(c) of the 1996 Regulations

and tear on clothing, bedding or the fabric of the home. The child may need to be closely supervised for his or her own safety or for the protection of others, or respite arrangements may be needed. The provision of specialist assistance, such as attending psychotherapy or visits to clinics, may result in additional expenditure for the adopters.

Regulation 3(2)(d)
of the 1996 Regulations

(d) if at the time of the placement for the adoption the child is mentally or physically disabled, or suffering from emotional or behavioural difficulties, but does not require additional expenditure at the time of placement, an adoption allowance may be paid at a later date because he or she requires more care and greater expenditure than were required at the time he or she was placed for adoption. This might be because there is a deterioration in the child's health or condition, or because of the increase in his or her age.

Regulation 3(2)(e)
of the 1996 Regulations

(e) if at the time of the placement for adoption it is known that there is a high risk that the child will develop an illness or disability and as a result at a later date he or she will require more care and greater expenditure of resources than were required at the time he or she was placed for adoption because such illness or disability occurs.

Regulation 3(3)
of the 1996 Regulations

160.   If it transpires, after a child has been placed with adopters, that the circumstances outlined in (c) or (d) above applied at the time the child was placed, an allowance can be paid.

161.   It will often be evident to the agency, before prospective adopters are identified, that an allowance may be needed because of one or more of the above factors is present. Where the agency considers that an allowance may become payable, in principle, because of the child's circumstances, it should record this information. It will be helpful if the agency's social workers undertaking the task of finding suitable adopters (or any other agency involved in finding adopters) know that payment of an adoption allowance will be considered, subject to the circumstances of the prospective adopter.

Linking the child and adopters: the place of the adoption allowance

162.   Once prospective adopters have been found for a child for whom, in principle, an adoption allowance may be paid, the adoption panel will need to make two recommendations

- whether adoption by these particular adopters would be in the best interests of the child, and

- whether an adoption allowance is needed to make the placement practicable.

163.   The child's need for permanence and security should always be the prime consideration in the selection of adopters. If particular adopters are the ones most likely to meet a child's needs, the fact there may be other adopters available who would not be eligible for an allowance is not relevant to the decision-making.

164.   Entitlement to an allowance does not automatically follow if the child's circumstances satisfy one or more of the conditions specified in the Regulations.

There may be occasions where, after the agency has decided that an allowance may be payable in principle, payment of the allowance cannot be justified after taking account of the adopters' financial circumstances. In addition, some prospective adopters may prefer to assume, unaided, the responsibility for meeting the child's needs and feel able to do so, even though they otherwise might have been eligible for an allowance.

Assessing the amount of the allowance

165.   The 1996 Regulations set broad parameters within which an assessment should be made. However, the amount of allowance payable in individual cases is a matter for the agency to determine, taking account of the child's needs and resources and the adopters' financial circumstances. Assessment of the various factors calls for careful and sensitive judgement. In assessing the amount of allowance the aim is to assist a successful placement and to enhance the child's well-being in the adoptive home. In undertaking its assessment the agency will need to look forward and consider all the financial circumstances which are likely to apply when the child is living in the adoptive home. It will need to consider

Regulation 4
of the 1996 Regulations

    (a)   the financial resources available to adopters

        The assessment of any adoption allowance must take account of the financial resources available to the adopters, including any financial benefit which would be available in respect of the child after adoption. Factors will include any projected earnings available to the adopters and significant income from capital investments. The value of the adopters' home should not be included. Any known financial benefit which the child will bring to the adoptive home, should be considered. However any disability living allowance or attendance allowance which the child receives (or subsequently becomes entitled to) should not be included as a source of income. Where an adoption allowance is payable, the adopters are entitled to claim Child Benefit from the date of placement for adoption. Child Benefit should be taken fully into account in determining the financial resources available, except where the adopters are receiving income support when Child Benefit is taken fully into account in the income support assessment. In such a case, the agency should disregard Child Benefit until the adopters cease to receive income support.

Regulation 4(2)(a)
of the 1996 Regulations

    (b)   the amount needed by adopters

        The amount needed by the adopters for their reasonable outgoings and commitments (excluding potential outgoings in respect of the child) needs to be assessed. The assessment should take into consideration expenses and outgoings which are familiar and accepted items of family expenditure. Factors for consideration will include housing and daily living expenses, transport costs, expenses related to children who are already part of the adoptive home, family outings and holidays. Adopters should be encouraged to give as many details as possible in respect of their outgoings so that the adoption does not lead to financial hardship or success of the placement being jeopardised because of financial difficulties.

Regulation 4(2)(b)
of the 1996 Regulations

    (c)   the financial needs and resources of the child

        The financial needs and resources of the child should also be taken into account. The agency should consider all factors, including everyday financial

Regulation 4(2)(c)
of the 1996 Regulations

needs, as well as any special needs and expenses related to the child's individual circumstances. Examples of special needs include special diet, replacement bedding and clothing resulting from heavy usage, transport costs associated with medical treatment, or transport costs to school, not otherwise available from the local education department. Occasionally, there will be circumstances in which the child has financial resources other than social security benefits payable in respect of him or her. This might, for example, include income arising from a capital investment or trust fund which can be considered by the agency as part of its assessment.

Regulation 4(3) of the 1996 Regulations

166.   The amount of allowance payable must not include any element of reward or profit for the care of the child by the adopters. The allowance should be governed by costs arising from any additional needs related to the child's circumstances. The amount of the allowance should not exceed the amount of the fostering allowance (including any enhancements payable solely in respect of the child's needs but excluding any element of reward) which would have been payable if the child were fostered by the adopters. In determining the amount, the agency should have regard to the child's age. Enhancements to the fostering allowance for special occasions such as Christmas, birthdays and holidays may be consolidated into the weekly adoption allowance.

Procedures for determining whether an allowance should be paid

Regulation 5(3) of the 1996 Regulations

167.   An approved adoption society which does not normally pay allowances is not required to consider whether an allowance may be paid or supply information concerning adoption allowances to adopters. It needs to comply with sub-paragraphs (c), (d) and (e) of regulation 5(1) which are outlined below only if they have considered whether or not to pay an allowance to adopters.

168.   The following paragraphs deal mainly with the procedure to be followed by local authorities when they are determining whether an allowance will be paid under the 1996 Regulations. (The procedure to follow when determining whether payment will continue under a revoked scheme is outlined in paragraphs 185-187 below).

Regulation 5(1) of the 1996 Regulations

169.   Prospective adopters should be given advice and information about the principles underlying adoption allowances, as well as information relating to the calculation of allowances and the arrangements with regard to review, variation and termination of allowances. Where prospective adopters are likely to be eligible for an allowance it is helpful if they complete adoption allowance assessment forms prior to the link with a child unless they do not wish to receive an allowance. This means that if a link with a child whose circumstances may attract an allowance is recommended by the adoption panel, information is available to the panel on the prospective adopter's eligibility for an allowance and the amount for which he or she would be eligible.

170.   The agency should notify the adopters in writing of its decision about whether any allowance is payable and, if so, the proposed amount. It is helpful if the adopters are given this information as part of the agency's written proposals in respect of the adoption. The notification to the adopters should specify the period of time during which the adopter may consider the agency's proposals and make any representations to the agency. Sufficient opportunity should be provided for the adopters to consider carefully the agency's proposals whilst not unduly postponing the date of placement.

Regulation 5(4) of the 1996 Regulations

A period of twenty-eight days from the time the proposal was sent to the applicants is suggested. However, where the assessment has been undertaken, in principle, beforehand, most prospective adopters will respond much more quickly so that the placement is not delayed. After considering any representations the agency should reach its final decision with regard to the allowance.

171. It is not necessary for the agency to reach a decision about the amount of allowance payable in cases where payment of an allowance is subject to developments in the child's condition which may occur after placement. In such cases, however, the agency should ensure that adopters are aware, before placement, of the conditions on which any adoption allowance will be made, including how the allowance will be assessed and arrangements for review, variation and termination (see paragraphs 178-182 below). Such adopters should be advised to contact the agency in the event of any deterioration in the child's circumstances to enable the agency to determine whether an allowance is now payable.

Regulation 5(2) of the 1996 Regulations

172. Where an approved adoption society is providing a prospective adopter for a child being placed by a local authority, the agency with legal responsibility for the child should decide whether an allowance is payable in respect of the particular placement and will be responsible for making the payments.

Notifications about adoption allowances to adopters

173. Once the agency has made a decision to pay an allowance, the agency must provide information about the allowance to the adopters. The information must be given in writing It is for agencies to determine their own arrangements for payment.

Regulation 6 of the 1996 Regulations

174. The information to be included is as follows

- the method by which the adoption allowance has been determined
- the amount of allowance to be paid to the adopters
- the date on which the first payment will be made
- the method by which the allowance will be paid, the frequency of payments and the period of payment
- the arrangements and procedures for review, variation and termination of the allowance
- the responsibilities of the adopters with regard to their agreement to notify the agency of changes in their circumstances or those of the child.

175. The conditions relating to changes of circumstance must be agreed by the adopters before an allowance is payable. The adopters are required to inform the agency immediately if

Regulation 3(4) of the 1996 Regulations

- the child ceases to have his or her home with the adopters, i.e. if the child's departure from the family home is regarded by the adopters as a permanent departure
- the family move, so that the agency can continue to issue payments to the correct address, and also because there may be a need to reassess the level of allowance
- the child dies

- there is any significant change in their financial circumstances or in the child's financial needs or resources.

176. The agency will need to operate with sensitivity in determining how far changes in financial circumstances or needs affect the allowance payable. It may, for example, be inappropriate to offset cost of living earnings increases against the adoption allowance although marked increases may be taken into consideration. Any marked deterioration in the child's condition leading to extra expenditure for the adopters may justify an increased allowance following reassessment.

177. Similar conditions apply when the allowance is reviewed annually. Before the allowance is payable, the adopters should agree to complete and supply to the agency an annual statement of their financial circumstances and the child's financial circumstances, including financial needs.

Review, variation and termination of allowances

Regulation 7
of the 1996 Regulations

178. Once payment has commenced the agency is required to review the allowance as follows

- annually after receiving a statement from the adopters giving information about their financial circumstances, the child's needs and resources, their address, and whether the child still has his or her home with them

- at any other time, when the agency is notified of any significant change in the adopters' or child's circumstances.

179. The purpose of the review is to ascertain whether there is a need for the allowance to continue and if so whether it should be maintained at the same level, increased, or reduced. The adopters are required to complete and submit to the agency an annual statement of their circumstances. It will be helpful if the agency

Regulation 7(2)
of the 1996 Regulations

triggers this by sending out a review form annually to adopters in receipt of allowances. If the adopters fail to return the form the agency may suspend the allowance until such time as the statement is supplied. Agencies should ensure that adopters are made aware of this provision by including it in the formal notification to adopters about adoption allowances.

180. For the purposes of the 1996 Regulations, once the adoption order is made relations between the adopters and the adoption agency exist only in respect of the allowance. The status of the child in law, in relation to the parents, is exactly the same as that of any child born to that family. Provision of any post-adoption support is independent from the administration of adoption allowances; neither is conditional upon the other. There is no requirement or expectation that the agency should visit the adopters once the adoption order has been made. Notification of changes of circumstances and the annual review of the allowance do not normally necessitate face to face contact between the agency and the adopters. These can normally be dealt with on an administrative basis, unless adopters wish to make representations about any alteration in their allowance.

Regulation 7(4) and (5)
of the 1996 Regulations

181. The circumstances, in which the agency shall terminate the allowance, are as follows

- where the child ceases to have a home with one or both of the adopters. This applies where the child's departure from the adoptive home is considered to be permanent. It does not apply to periods of temporary absence away from the adoptive home for example, in connection with education, respite care or hospitalisation

- where the child ceases full-time education and commences employment or qualifies for a place on a Government training scheme

- where the child qualifies for income support or a jobseeker's allowance in his or her own right

- where the child reaches the age of eighteen, unless he or she remains in full-time education. In such a case, the allowance may continue until the child reaches the age of twenty-one so long as he or she continues in full-time education

- where a predetermined period agreed between the agency and the adopters expires.

182.   The 1996 Regulations do not provide for an adoption allowance to recommence once it has been terminated. It is important, therefore, that payments should be described as suspended rather than terminated where circumstances other than those set out in the preceeding paragraph apply eg where there has been an increase in the adopter's income.

Date of payment

183.   Where all the conditions specified in the 1996 Regulations have been satisfied and the agency has decided that an allowance should be paid, the payment of the allowance should start from the date the child is placed for adoption or from a later date determined by the adoption agency. Where a foster placement has become an adoption placement the agency and the adopters should clearly understand and agree the date of the adoption placement from which the payment is to commence. The adopters must be notified in writing of the date payment is to begin, the amount and how it is to be paid.

Regulation 3(5) of the 1996 Regulations

184.   Where an agreement is made in principle to pay an allowance after the adoption order is made, the adopters and the agency must understand and agree that the allowance will only be payable in respect of the child's needs. For example, an allowance will not become payable because of a change relating to the adopters' circumstances which is unrelated to the child's condition, such as the loss of a job.

Adoptive parents in receipt of an adoption allowance under a revoked scheme

185.   Transitional provisions will allow agencies to pay an allowance to

- adopters who, before the Regulations came into force on 1 April 1998, were receiving an allowance under a scheme which has been revoked by section 51B of the 1978 Act and who agree to receive an allowance complying with the Regulations

- adopters in respect of whom the agency had agreed that an allowance would be payable under a revoked scheme subject to the satisfaction of any particular condition. This would apply, for example, where the agency had agreed in principle to pay an allowance subject to a deterioration in the child's health.

186.   Agencies should contact all adopters who are

- receiving a payment under a revoked scheme

- in respect of whom payment under a revoked scheme had been agreed in principle subject to particular conditions being satisfied or subject to an adoption order being made.

187.   The agency should inform such adopters about the terms and conditions which apply to allowances made under the 1996 Regulations including information as to how such allowances are determined and the annual review. The information should include an indication of the amount of any allowance which the adopters would receive under the 1996 Regulations. This may, of course, be the same as their existing allowance. Particular care should be taken to ensure that adopters are made aware of any benefits or disadvantages which may arise from a transfer to the 1996 Regulations. The adopters should be asked to specify whether they would prefer their payments to continue under the revoked scheme or whether they wish to be paid under the 1996 Regulations. Adopters may find it helpful to discuss their position in person with a social worker or a member of administrative staff. Adopters who are receiving an allowance, or for whom an allowance has been agreed, in respect of a child whose circumstances fall outwith the Regulations can still continue to receive or be eligible for an allowance under the revoked scheme.

Adoption Case Records

Establishment and storage of records

Regulation 23   188.   A confidential adoption case record must be set up in respect of any child or adopter who comes within the scope of the Regulations. Any reports, recommendations or decisions made by the agency should be stored or recorded on the file. The details of any recommendation or decision about an adoption allowance, including cases where the agency decides that no allowance is payable, should be included. Where a child was looked after prior to the decision to place him or her for adoption, it is necessary to open a new case record once the decision has been made that adoption is in his or her best interests.

189.   All adoption records where an adoption order is made and the indexes to all the case records must be stored in a place of special security for at least seventy-five years. The record or index may be preserved on computer or microfilm, provided the total record can be reproduced. The conditions in which the records are stored must be conducive to preservation for seventy-five years. Other records to do with adoption should also be stored in a place of special security for as long as the agency considers appropriate. Where a child continues to be looked after because an adoption order is not made the record needs to be kept for seventy-five years from the child's date of birth.

Access to records

Regulation 24(1)   190.   The records are highly confidential. The only exceptions to the confidentiality requirement are that access must be given

- to those holding an inquiry under section 6A of the Social Work (Scotland) Act 1968, for the purposes of such an inquiry

- to the Secretary of State

- to the Commissioner for Local Administration in Scotland appointed under section 24 of the Local Government (Scotland) Act 1975 for the purpose of any investigation conducted under Part II of the Act

- to the persons and authorities referred to in other parts of the Regulations but only the extent specified in those Regulations

- to a court in a freeing for adoption or adoption application

- to a Curator ad Litem or Reporting Officer appointed in an adoption or freeing for adoption case.

191.   An adoption agency may provide such access to its case records and the indexes to them and disclose such information in its possession, as it considers appropriate either for the purposes of carrying out its functions as an adoption agency or to a person who is authorised in writing by the Secretary of State to obtain information for the purposes of research. *Regulation 24(2)*

192.   A written record must be kept by an adoption agency of any access provided to case records or disclosure made. *Regulation 24(3)*

193.   Provisions for access to records by adopted adults are discussed in paragraphs 225-227 below.

Contact in Adoption

The nature and management of contact

194.   A significant change in adoption practice over recent years has been the recognition that, in some instances, a birth parent or a member of the birth family, should have a continuing role in an adopted child's life.

195.   Although it is possible for contact arrangements to be specified as part of an adoption order, this is rarely done in practice. Thus, most arrangements are reliant on the adoptive parents willingly accepting and carrying them through once the order is granted.

196.   Birth parents are now much more likely to have been part of the agency's process of selecting adoptive parents and may also have met them prior to the placement. A meeting can help both adopters and birth parents achieve a realistic, and often more sympathetic, view of each other. This can aid the adopters at a later stage when telling the child about his or her parents and why he or she was placed for adoption.

197.   An assessment of whether any form of contact should be retained must be based solely on what is likely to be in the child's interests, both at the point of placement and in the future. The views of the adoptive parents will be important as they will have the responsibility, once the adoption order is made, of managing the contact between the child and the birth parents. There will be some situations where the circumstances which led to the adoption are such that contact of any

kind will be ruled out and many others where only indirect contact will be appropriate.

198.   There are a number of ways in which contact between the birth parent, the child and the adoptive family can be maintained and the form of contact between them may change over the years. Letter-writing and exchange of photographs are the most common. It is often helpful for the child if the arrangement can be a reciprocal one so that the adoptive parents are also receiving information about the birth parent. This may take place directly between the families or may be facilitated by an adoption agency acting as an intermediary. Exchange of written information often proves, in practice, to be more than just an administrative arrangement for the agency. Agencies may be asked by adopters to become involved to deal with dilemmas and questions which arise, such as

- how adopters should tell the child about the arrangement

- whether the child should be directly involved when he or she is old enough to write to the birth parent

- if, when the child is old enough to appreciate the significance of the arrangement, he or she does not want it to continue

- if the adopters do not want the arrangements to continue.

All parties need to be prepared for such contingencies and need to understand that the arrangements may need to change over time.

Regulation 11(2)(b)   199.   If the adoption panel recommends that there should be continuing contact following an adoption between a child and one or both birth parents, the Panel must provide a written report to the agency as to why adoption is recommended rather than an alternative course of action. The report should indicate why, in these circumstances, adoption was considered to be in the interests of the child rather than an order which did not sever his or her legal relationship with birth parents. Occasionally, having taken the child's views into account, the agency may reach a decision that a placement for adoption, where some face to face contact with parents is retained, is in the child's interests. Generally, the agency would be involved in establishing contact arrangements and, at times, may have a part to play in any continuing contact. In some cases this would be arranged directly between the birth parent and the adopters. Once an adoption order is made this would be a matter for the adopters to decide. Whatever arrangements are made, they must continue to be in the best interests of the child.

200.   As a child who is having contact with a birth parent grows older, there may come a time when he or she no longer wants a particular form of contact or any form of contact. In such instances, the adopters will have to decide whether the child's best interests will be served by trying to arrange for contact to be maintained in some other way; for example, by letter between them and the birth parents or whether the restriction or termination of contact is more appropriate. This will be a matter for adopters to decide.

Wider family contact

201.   Sibling contact is often very important where siblings are not placed together. When children are very young, the significance of the sibling relationship

may not be apparent but its importance often increases as the child grows up. Adoptive parents need to be willing to accept the responsibility placed on them to maintain the relationship. Often contact is arranged between the adoptive families themselves, but sometimes there may be siblings who remain with the birth family and the agency may remain involved in facilitating contact under these circumstances.

202.   Where other relatives, such as grandparents, have had a significant and positive relationship with the child, the appropriateness of continuing contact should be considered by the agency. The considerations concerning contact outlined in paragraphs 194-200 above may also be applicable to wider family contact.

Step-parent and Family Adoption

The legal context

203.   About half of the adoption orders granted in Scotland at present are step-family adoptions and this is often seen by families as an appropriate way of formalising relationships and of giving the step-parent parental responsibilities. On some occasions, other family members may apply to adopt a child for whom they are caring. All these applicants are required to notify the local authority of their intention to apply for an adoption order. The local authority is required to investigate the circumstances and submit a report to the court.

Section 22

204.   The social worker has a duty to assess whether adoption will safeguard and promote the child's welfare throughout his or her life. If the child is subject to a supervision requirement, the local authority is also required to notify the Principal Reporter.

Section 6(1)(a)

Section 73(5) of the 1995 Act

205.   It is often difficult for families to understand why the local authority has to carry out an assessment of their circumstances when one partner is the birth parent of the child. The local authority should provide written information for step-families and other family members considering adoption, about the service which they provide and their statutory duties.

Implications of step-parent adoption

206.   Adoption severs all legal links which exist between the child, the birth parent who is no longer a member of the family and his or her extended family. These family members may be very significant to the child. The seriousness of taking this irrevocable step and its implications for the child as he or she grows up should not be underestimated. The feelings of loss which are experienced by some adopted adults may also apply to those adopted in step-families. Although they have the advantage of living with a birth parent, it is not always easy for them to get information about or maintain contact with their other birth parent. Even where the other birth parent is dead, contact with his or her extended family will often remain important.

207.   Step-families decide to pursue adoption for a number of reasons

- to legally change the child's name so that everyone in the family has the same name

- to ensure that the child has the same rights of inheritance as any children of the marriage

- as a way of making a full commitment to the child

- as a means of obtaining parental responsibilities so that if anything happens to the partner who is the legal parent, the child's future is safeguarded.

208.   As in any adoption application, the court must consider whether there is a better practicable alternative to adoption for the child and the social worker's report will need to cover this issue. It is therefore important that other means which might achieve their aims, short of adoption are discussed with the applicants. This could include the child being included in the step-parent's will, or an application for a residence order by the parent and the step-parent.

Section 14(1B)   209.   Anyone who is aged over twenty-one and is married to a birth parent who is over eighteen and has parental rights and responsibilities in respect of a child can apply to adopt that child. The birth parent no longer has to apply to adopt his or her own child. The applicant must notify the local authority of his or her intention to adopt and both birth parents are required to give agreement (where the birth father has parental responsibilities) or have their agreement dispensed with.

210.   The social worker should explain to the family what will be involved in the investigation of their circumstances. He or she should establish why the family has chosen to pursue adoption. By this time it is often hard to counsel applicants about the merits of other options, but it is good professional practice that these are explored.

Implications of adoption by other family members

Section 11   211.   Occasionally a local authority may receive notification of an intention to apply for an adoption order from family members other than the step-parents, often grandparents, an aunt or an uncle. The 1978 Act gives a definition of relative which covers a grandparent, brother, sister, uncle or aunt whether "*of the full blood*

Section 65   *or half blood or by affinity*" and includes, where the father of the child was not married to the mother, the father or any other person who would be a relative within the meaning of this definition if the father were married to the mother.

212.   Adoption by family members can be complicated for the child to understand and can create complex relationships. For example, if the adoption is by a grandparent, the birth mother then becomes the sister of the child. Counselling in such situations is important if the family are to appreciate the possible implications of the adoption for the child's future. The possible advantages for the child of pursuing other options, such as a residence order, should be discussed with the family.

213.   The formal process of the adoption is the same as for step-parent adoptions.

The local authority report

Section 22   214.   Once the notification has been received, the local authority has a duty to investigate and report to the court on the circumstances of the applicant to determine his or her suitability as an adoptive parent, and on whether the welfare of the child

would be promoted by adoption throughout his or her life. This report will normally *Section 6*
be expected by the court within twelve weeks.

215.   Local authorities should consider whether they need to make checks as they would for other adoptive applicants, although this can only be done with the consent of the applicants. A full medical is not necessary but the agency should consider writing to the applicants' GPs to ask if there are any medical issues which are pertinent to the adoption application. The agency medical adviser may be consulted for advice. In circumstances where the applicants refuse to consent to checks being made this fact should be noted in the report for the court. The local authority should in particular check that the placement has not been made in contravention of section 11 i.e. that the arrangements for the adoption were not made illegally.

216.   The social worker should consider the child's views about the adoption. If *Section 6* the child is aged twelve years or over his or her formal agreement will be required if he or she is capable of giving it. This will be obtained by the reporting officer. Occasionally, the social worker may come across a situation where the child believes that the step-parent is the birth parent or where the parent and step-parent refuse to allow the child to be made aware of why the social worker is there. With a young child, it may be relevant to discuss with the petitioners how they intend to explain to the child about adoption and advise them on possible ways of doing this. In families where the child is older, the social worker should advise the family that the situation will be discussed in his or her report to the court.

217.   Any parent who has parental rights and responsibilities will be required to *Section 16* agree to the adoption, and, if he or she does not agree, his or her agreement will have to be dispensed with. In cases where there is, or has been, an established relationship between the child and the birth father, who does not have parental rights, the social worker should consider whether to contact him and ascertain his views about the proposed adoption. His views should be noted in the report and may have a bearing on whether a recommendation is made that adoption is in the best interests of the child.

218.   The report to the court and the court process are described in paragraphs 268-275 below.

Post-adoption Support and Services for Adopted Adults

The duty to provide services

219.   There is a duty on adoption agencies to provide post-adoption support services *Section 1* for children, adopters, anyone else with a problem related to adoption such as birth parents, and services for adopted adults. Agencies should provide post-adoption services in ways which are supportive to those involved and which can be easily accessed without undue delay. This is an area of work where partnerships between *Section 1(3)* local authorities and adoption societies are often beneficial. Local authorities should provide details of their post-adoption services in their children's services plans.

Provision of post-adoption services for children, their adopters and their birth parents

220.   Children being placed for adoption may have suffered significant emotional damage as a result of their earlier experiences and adoptive parents can expect to

face a range of emotional and behavioural problems. Long-term support may be required in some cases to help sustain families through the remainder of the adoptee's childhood and to early adulthood. For others, help may be required at a particular stage. For example, adolescence is a crucial time for adoptive placements and a significant number of placements become troubled or disrupt at this stage, even among those children who were placed as babies. Ongoing contact arrangements may mean the agency's continuing involvement. Birth parents may also require support at various times after the adoption order is granted.

221.   The availability of post-adoption support should be mentioned to families at the preparation stage so that it is seen as an integral part of the adoption service rather than as something which they can only seek at times when they are experiencing severe problems. It should not be perceived by families as something which has connotations of failure.

222.   In step-parent adoptions, as in other adoptions, local authorities have a duty to provide counselling and assistance to the adopted child, to the adoptive parent, or counselling to other persons if they have problems relating to adoption. Social workers should inform families that they can seek assistance if they need it in the future and should provide them with a copy of the agency's information on post-adoption services.

223.   Agencies should be flexible in considering how to meet the needs of adoptive families and a range of options needs to be developed. Some options are

-   provision of practical help. For example a home help may be needed to allow adopters to give sufficient time and attention to a large family group or a disabled child

-   self-help groups are an acceptable and accessible form of support for many adoptive parents and it is in the interests of agencies to promote their development locally. Adopters should also be given information about any national organisations or groups such as Parent to Parent Information on Adoption Services (PPIAS)

-   some agencies provide training for adoptive parents which builds on their experience or addresses particular issues which they may be facing. These can include talking to their child about adoption, issues related to adolescence or issues about caring for a child who has been sexually abused. Agencies may wish to co-operate to develop such training or consider paying for adopters to attend training provided by other organisations

-   advice, counselling or support should be readily available, preferably from a social worker experienced in adoption matters

-   for some families, planned respite services will be necessary to allow them to cope with the level of difficulty or disability which their child presents. Some adoptive parents will have extended family or friends who can provide such breaks but others will need respite services provided by the agency including possibly short-term provision of accommodation.

Provision of services for adopted adults

224.   A number of adults who have been adopted seek information about the circumstances of their adoption and about their birth parents and relatives. The

local authority or adoption agency is obliged to provide counselling for people who have received information about their birth records and who apply for counselling. The Children Act 1989 provides that adopted people living in the United Kingdom who apply for birth records information can choose to receive counselling from the local authority in the area in which they live. This means, for example, that someone who was adopted in England but is now living in Scotland, and who has applied for his or her birth records information to the Registrar General for England and Wales, can receive the information via his or her local authority in Scotland. Where an adopted adult who is seeking information lives abroad, there is no obligation on him or her to receive counselling but he or she may wish to do so. Department of Health leaflets ACR 101 and 114 provide helpful information.

Access to records by adopted adults

225. In Scotland, adopted people have had a right of access to their birth records since 1930 and any adopted person aged 16 or over is entitled to information about, or a copy or extract of, their original birth entry. There is no obligation on the adopted person to seek counselling and it is not a precondition of obtaining information. However, when adopted people apply for their original birth certificate, the Registrar General will advise them that counselling services are available from the local authority for the area in which they live or, if their adoption was arranged by an adoption agency, from that agency. *Section 45(5)*

226. The adopted adult has a right to see the papers relating to the court process in his or her adoption and these can be obtained by applying to the court which granted the adoption order, i.e. the court within whose jurisdiction the adoptive parents lived at the time of the adoption. These papers may, however, have been transferred to the Scottish Records Office in Edinburgh. These papers include the reports of the Curator ad Litem and the Reporting Officer and now would also contain the report prepared under section 22 or section 23 of the 1978 Act. While these records do not always contain a great deal of information, they can be useful in identifying for adopted adults which adoption agency, if any, was involved in arranging their adoption.

227. Adopted adults may also want information from adoption agency records. Such information may be supplied to the adopted adult or to the local authority where the adopted person lives, if he or she has applied to them for counselling. However, in the past a large number of adoptions were arranged privately through for example a lawyer, a minister or a doctor and it is often difficult for adopted adults in private adoptions to find any records apart from the court records. Other adopted adults may learn that their adoption was arranged through one of the many voluntary adoption societies which no longer exist but they may be able to trace some records if that agency had arranged for their records to be kept by another adoption agency. Information about the location and existence of records can be obtained from the Scottish Adoption Registry held by Family Care. Adoption agencies which cease to exist are obliged to ensure that their records are transferred to another adoption agency. *Regulation 25*

Regulation 26

Seeking information and searching for birth parents or relatives

228. There are varied reasons why adopted adults seek information about their origins. This can vary from curiosity, to a practical need for medical or other

information, to a much deeper need to resolve questions about their own identity. Many will have had a happy childhood and enjoy satisfying relationships with their adoptive parents. Others will have found their adoptive upbringing less satisfactory. Agencies should be aware of the need to pass information to the adoptive parent for their adopted child as he or she grows up.

229.   Counselling is often a very important part of the process for an adopted person. Adopted people should be enabled to talk freely about their experience of adoption and to reach a decision, both about whether they wish access to the information in their adoption records and then about whether they wish to try and trace a birth parent or relative. Counselling should enable adopted people to clarify their feelings about their adoption and about their expectations of their birth family. Adopted people may need to be prepared that the circumstances of their birth family could be very different from that of their adopted family and they may need to express their doubts and fears about what the adoption records may contain if they can be traced.

230.   Sometimes there will be original correspondence or even photographs in the agency record. Having these may be far more important to the adopted adult than to the agency and agencies should use their discretion in removing such personal items from the file to give to the adopted adult and replace them with a photocopy. If agencies are considering microfilming or computerising records, it is very important that such original documents are extracted and preserved.

231.   Adopted people should be encouraged to carry out as much as possible of the search for information themselves. This allows them to retain control over what happens and, in particular, about how far or how fast to go. The agency's role is to give advice and practical support where necessary and to help adopted people come to terms with the information they discover. It is important throughout that the motivation to pursue such a search comes from the adopted person and not from anyone else, such as a partner.

232.   Adopted people may have strong feelings about some of the information they are given. It may be that the information repeated some very painful details with which they have to come to terms. For adopted people who were placed some time ago, counselling may have to bridge the gap between then and now in terms of the social mores of the time; for example, helping the adopted person to appreciate that single parents have not been an accepted part of society for very long. The counsellor may have to help the adopted person deal with the fact that no records of the adoption can be traced, either because it was a private adoption, or because the agency has since closed and perhaps destroyed its records, as was the case with some agencies which operated in Scotland.

233.   Once he or she has collected whatever information he or she can, then the adopted person will decide whether or not he or she wishes to search for a birth parent or relative. Some will decide not to pursue a search, others will take a long time to consider what they have learned before making a decision. It is important that adopted people are prepared for a number of eventualities if they decide to search. They have to understand the implications that the search may have for their birth parent or relative and that they may face a rejection if they find them. Most birth parents or relatives are happy to have contact but for a few, it may be too painful or their personal circumstances may not allow it. Some adopted adults may not be able to find their birth parent or relative so that their search becomes increasingly frustrating. Sometimes contact may be established through the Birthlink

Adoption Contact Register for Scotland (based at Family Care) or through information placed on the child's record by a birth parent or relative. This means that the adopted adult will know whether or not his or her contact will be welcomed.

234.   It is suggested that the first contact with the birth parent or relative is made by the adoption agency social worker. This is for a number of reasons

- preserving the confidentiality of both parties

- allowing the agency to check that it is the right person

- allowing the birth parent or relative to come to terms with the information that his or her child or relation wishes to see him or her and the agency can assess the birth parent or relative's readiness for such contact

- providing the birth parent or relative with someone to talk to about his or her feelings about the adoption which may be rekindled

- giving the agency the opportunity to bridge the gap for both parties. Birth parents or relatives may only be able to remember the baby or child they had; adopted people may have little or no memory of a birth parent or relative

- allowing the agency to clarify that the objectives of the contact for each are clear to the other; for example, if adopted people visualise a one-off meeting to clarify issues for themselves and to reassure the birth parents or relatives that they have been happy, the birth parents or relatives need to be aware of this and not anticipate ongoing contact.

235.   Adoptive parents may find the process of their son or daughter searching for birth parents or relatives difficult and often the adopted person decides not to tell them. This obviously has the risk that they will find out by accident or that the adopted person starts to deceive them. Adopted people should be encouraged and supported to tell their parents, although this must remain their decision. If the adopted person decides to tell his or her parents it can be helpful for the parents to talk through their feelings with the agency to deal with their concerns about their son or daughter's search.

236.   Sometimes agencies may be approached by young people under the age of sixteen looking for information about their birth family. Children under sixteen have no legal right of access to personal records so counselling in such situations is important in order to explore the issues which have brought the young person to the agency. With the young person's consent, it will usually be appropriate to inform their parents that they are searching for information and involve them in the information-giving process.

237.   Those who undertake the complex and skilled task of counselling adopted adults should be experienced in adoption work and in counselling and should be offered specific training and support. Small agencies may wish to consider joint training or consultancy.

Inter-country Adoption

Scotland's approach to inter-country adoption

238.   There has been a gradual increase in the numbers of children from abroad being brought to Scotland for adoption, usually from developing countries, or those

which have undergone a political upheaval, experienced war or a natural disaster. As the number of babies and young children available for adoption has declined in Scotland, some prospective adopters have looked to other countries for a young child to adopt. Others respond to publicity about the difficult circumstances of children in particular countries and wish to save a child from a situation in which they perceive children are suffering harm.

239.   Scotland's approach to inter-country adoption is influenced by the provisions of the 1986 United Nations Declaration on Adoption and Fostering. This Declaration provides that international adoption

- may be in the best interests of the child who cannot be cared for in a suitable manner in his or her own country

- that the child's welfare must be the primary consideration

- that safeguards equivalent to those which apply in national adoption are applied to inter-country adoption to protect the welfare of the children concerned.

240.   Local authorities have a vital role to play in safeguarding the welfare of children who come from overseas for adoption. This includes

- advising and counselling those who are considering adopting children from overseas

- assessing the suitability of prospective adopters

- supervising the child's welfare and making reports and recommendations to the court when a child arrives from overseas for adoption.

241.   In addition to being the first step in securing the welfare of the child, professional advice and counselling are vital for people who are considering adoption from overseas. They need to understand and address the particular implications for the child and themselves, in both the short and long-term, of adopting a child from a different country, a different culture, and sometimes a different race, who may have suffered great early disadvantage, and often, with little, if any, information about the child's background and history. It is helpful for people considering inter-country adoption if local authorities provide written information for them outlining these issues, the adoption process, any charges that will be made and the service that will be provided.

The inter-country adoption process

242.   The general procedure for seeking admission of a child for adoption in the UK is set out in the Home Office leaflet RON 117. Adoption agencies and prospective adopters can obtain copies from the Immigration and Nationality Directorate, Home Office, Lunar House, Croydon CR9 2BY - telephone 0181 686 0688. Prospective adopters seeking help should be given information about the entry clearance procedures or advised to contact the Home Office at the above number.

243.   It is for the Home Office to determine whether a child from a non-designated country will be admitted to the UK following an application for Entry Clearance. If the Home Office is satisfied that there are no immigration reasons for refusal and

that the proposed adoption involves a genuine transfer of parental responsibility on the grounds of the parents' inability to care for the child, they will look to Social Work Services Group (SWSG) in The Scottish Office for advice on the welfare aspects of the proposed adoption.

244.   In giving advice SWSG needs to be satisfied on the following matters

    a.   that adoption is likely to be in the child's interests

    b.   the reasons for the proposed adoption; evidence of the child's identity and as much information about his or her circumstances, history and background as can be discovered, including a report on the BAAF inter-country medical form

    c.   that there is evidence that the child is legally available for adoption and that the appropriate authorities support the adoption plans and have authorised the child's departure from the country of origin for the purposes of adoption

    d.   there is either a valid parental agreement, in a form acceptable to a UK court and given freely and with full understanding of the effects of a UK adoption order, or official certification that the child has been genuinely abandoned and the parents cannot be found

    e.   that the prospective adopters are suitable adopters for a child from a particular country or countries.

245.   In order to be satisfied about a, b, c and d above, SWSG relies on reports from the authorities in the child's country of origin, supplemented where necessary by enquiries made by the Entry Clearance Officer in the child's country of origin and information provided by the prospective adopters. For e above, SWSG relies on the prospective adopters' local authority for a report and recommendation on their suitability, or otherwise, as adopters.

Assessment and reports

246.   When the Home Office seeks advice on an Entry Clearance application for an already identified child, SWSG requests the relevant local authority to provide a report on the prospective adopters. Because the identified child is often living in difficult circumstances, local authorities are asked, if possible, to provide reports within twelve weeks of receiving the request.

247.   However, applications in these circumstances are now rare and local authorities are increasingly asked by prospective adopters to prepare a report in advance of an Entry Clearance application and before a particular child has been offered to the adopters. There are many advantages in assessing families at an early stage and local authorities are asked to do so in all suitable cases. The relevant factors are

    •   more countries are now imposing official controls over inter-country adoption and will not accept applicants for consideration as adopters without a social work report and recommendation from a statutory agency. It is desirable that prospective adopters are encouraged to adopt from these countries where arrangements are most carefully controlled, where only reports from a statutory agency are acceptable and where compliance with procedures of both countries is assured

- it is advantageous to local authorities to take the opportunity of providing advice and information and of influencing arrangements at the earliest possible stage since, if a child is admitted for adoption, they will be responsible for supervising the welfare of the child and for providing section 22 reports to the court

- the process of assessment serves not only to check the general suitability of prospective adopters but to explore their motivation and their understanding of, and ability to deal with, foreseeable and unforeseen difficulties in the placement. Assessment and preparation can proceed more effectively when prospective adopters are not already committed to a particular child and there is pressure to complete the process because an early decision is needed

- it provides an opportunity to inform families who meet the agency's criteria of the children needing adoption in this country, so that they can make an informed choice about which type of adoption to pursue

- it may give families the opportunity to attend an adoption preparation group. Agencies may wish to consider collaborating to provide groups specifically for overseas adopters.

248.   It is important that reports prepared by local authorities are not misused by adopters to bring a child into the country in breach of the Entry Clearance procedures, when there will be no opportunity to investigate the circumstances of the placement or the child's background. Adopters must apply for and receive Entry Clearance before bringing a child into the country. Entry Clearance is not a formality which can be omitted simply because the prospective adopters have been found generally suitable to adopt a child from overseas. Investigation of the circumstances of the adoption arrangements in the child's country of origin and of the particular child's background and history is an essential part of the Entry Clearance procedure.

249.   From time to time prospective adopters are advised that they should not seek to adopt from certain countries. Prospective adopters should always be strongly advised not to seek to adopt through intermediaries who are not properly authorised by the overseas countries. SWSG can advise on the latest available information on a particular country or agency.

250.   Whether reports are prepared in advance of or in connection with an Entry Clearance application, they should be undertaken by social workers experienced in adoption and child placement work. SWSG commends the use of BAAF Form F as a basis for preparing the report. The content of the report and associated police and health checks and interviews with referees should follow the pattern established by good practice in respect of any other adoption. Recommendations should specify the age group, health and social characteristics of a child or children who the applicants might be suitable to adopt. It is important to indicate the length of time for which the report is valid. Approval should not be for an indefinite period.

251.   Reports should include an assessment of the applicant's suitability to adopt a child from another country and, where applicable, from a different religious, linguistic, cultural or racial background. Consideration should be given in the report to how the family intend to convey information to the child about his or her background (about which they may have very little information) and his or her country of origin, how they intend to have regard to the child's race, religion, culture,

and language, and how they will deal with racism or prejudice if this becomes an issue for the child or themselves.

252.   Agencies should consider whether their criteria for domestic adoptions (see paragraphs 62-70) also apply to overseas adoptions, although criteria applied solely to limit the number of adopters should not be applied to overseas adopters. However, those criteria which are concerned with safeguarding and promoting the welfare of children throughout their lives apply as much to overseas adoptions as to domestic adoptions. In this regard, age is a relevant factor and applicants should be expected to have the necessary health and vigour to bring up a child until adulthood and especially during the demanding years of adolescence. Where another country has its own stricter criteria these should be observed. Where it is decided not to accept an applicant for assessment they should be notified in writing.

253.   In inter-country adoption it is necessary to examine the possibility that the child may have health and developmental problems as he or she grows older. This is an important consideration in the assessment and preparation of prospective adopters.

254.   Agencies should refer prospective overseas adopters to their adoption panel. Panels may need to seek advice and training on overseas adoption so that they are aware of the particular issues involved. Where the assessment is carried out by an adoption society on behalf of a local authority, the adoption society may refer the case to their own adoption panel. However, all recommendations to SWSG concerning the suitability of overseas adopters must be made by the relevant local authority decision-maker. It should be noted that referral to the adoption panel will mean that the prospective adopters receive a copy of the home study report. It should be made clear on the report that completion of the report does not denote approval.

255.   Occasionally, prospective adopters themselves commission a home study report from social workers acting in a private capacity. Where such a report is made available to SWSG in connection with an Entry Clearance application, a copy is sent to the local authority, together with any other relevant information, when SWSG requests a report and recommendations from the local authority. It is for the local authority to decide whether, and to what extent, it makes use of the contents of a privately commissioned report as part of its own report of its assessment of the prospective adopters. No support should be given to the contents of private reports except where the local authority is satisfied, in the particular case, that it can fully accept the contents of the report.

256.   Local authorities are advised not to refer prospective adopters to private social workers in any circumstances except where such a social worker is commissioned and paid by the local authority to produce the report on the authority's behalf. Where a report is prepared by or on behalf of an adoption agency there will be no risk of a breach of section 11 and section 65(3) of the 1978 Act.

257.   It is open to local authorities to require prospective adopters to meet the costs of assessment, preparation of the report and the adoption panel, whether conducted by their own or commissioned staff. This enables authorities to commission adoption societies or freelance social workers in whom they have confidence, to do the work on their behalf. In these circumstances, a senior manager

in the local authority will need to ensure that health, police and other checks are carried out through local authority systems.

258.　Reports may be sent directly to the appropriate authority or agency overseas where it is known that they have proper safeguards and controls and where it is known that the authorities will not release the child until the requirements of both the countries have been met. In individual cases SWSG can advise local authorities on the countries and agencies to whom this might apply.

259.　Reports prepared by adoption agencies recommending people as UK adopters are only acceptable to SWSG in connection with Entry Clearance applications for inter-country adoptions if the local authority updates and augments the report to outline whether or not it is satisfied that the prospective adopters are also suitable to adopt a child from overseas. Approval as adopters in the UK cannot be automatically applied to inter-country adoption because of the special factors to be considered. There have, unfortunately, been instances of prospective adopters obtaining custody of a child and subsequently bringing the child into the UK without Entry Clearance, by making use either of a letter from an adoption agency stating that they have been approved as prospective adopters for a child in this country and placed on a waiting list, or by using reports prepared in accordance with the Adoption Agencies Regulations. Care should be taken to try to ensure that letters and/or reports are not used by prospective adopters to circumvent Entry Clearance procedures. Letters and reports should always state whether the decision or recommendations to approve relates to domestic adoptions or overseas adoptions.

Linking

260.　It is the nature of inter-country adoption that while counselling, assessment and preparation of adopters are the responsibility of the authorities in the UK, the linking of prospective adopters and children takes place in the children's country of origin. Local authorities will have no opportunity to influence these decisions. It is therefore of particular importance that, for the guidance of those who have the task of making or authorising placement, recommendations should be clear and specific about the age range and any particular characteristics of the child for whom the prospective adopters would be suitable or unsuitable.

261.　Where a report has been prepared in advance by a local authority and an Entry Clearance application is made subsequently for a particular child, SWSG will give the local authority all the relevant information which is available about the child. They will be asked, if appropriate, to up-date or confirm the previous recommendation in the light of the specific proposed child.

262.　At this stage, SWSG will decide whether they can recommend to the Home Office that the proposed adoption would be in the child's best interests and that SWSG can find no reason why a court in the UK would not make an adoption order. In reaching this decision, SWSG will have regard to all the information which has been gathered about the child, the prospective adopters and the circumstances of the proposed adoption.

Post-placement

263.　In the case of a child from a non-designated country, an adoption application must be made in the UK. The legislation requires that a child not related to his or her prospective adopters must live with them for a period of at least twelve months before an adoption order can be granted by a court. In the intervening period the placement should be treated as a private fostering arrangement under the Foster Children (Scotland) Act 1984 and the Foster Children (Private Fostering) (Scotland) Regulations 1985. This also applies where a child has been brought into the UK without prior Entry Clearance. SWSG will see that local authorities are advised of such cases as soon as notification is received from the Home Office. Local authorities are asked to notify SWSG of any cases which come to their attention before they are notified by SWSG.

Health issues

264.   As part of the Entry Clearance procedures, prospective adopters must arrange for a medical report on the child to be provided on the BAAF inter-country adoption medical form. Information about the health and development of children proposed for adoption in the UK is not required with a view to prohibiting the admission of children with health problems. It is an essential part of the UK adoption practice, and a legal requirement in relation to placements in the UK, that information is provided about health and development of children proposed for adoption. Prospective adopters must be fully appraised of any significant birth or early life experience that may affect the physical, emotional and mental development of the child so that they are aware of any associated responsibilities.

265.   Some children proposed for inter-country adoption face health and developmental difficulties, some children will require active treatment; many will need additional care and attention; in others, harmful experiences may lead to permanent physical or mental impairment. Prospective adopters must consider these risks, understand the implications for the child's care and be able to demonstrate that they have the capacity to deal with health and developmental problems, and with uncertainties about future development should they emerge.

266.   Some children who are being offered for adoption have been exposed to the risk of AIDS/HIV infection and also the risk of Hepatitis B, which is far more infectious. Adopters need to know that testing for HIV in young children is very unreliable. Neither a positive nor a negative test can be taken as a true indicator of the likelihood of the child developing AIDS. It is vital that social workers are fully aware of the impact on children who develop AIDS and the difficulties that such parents will have to endure. The true reality of caring for a child suffering from AIDS needs to be fully discussed with prospective adopters.

267.   Advice should be sought from the agency's medical adviser where health issues are of concern in a specific case. Medical advisers are also invaluable contributors if preparation groups are held for overseas adopters.

Services to the Courts

Statutory requirements

268.   In the field of adoption, the courts are the forum where final binding decisions are made about the future of the child. In order for this process to be effective, adoption agencies must ensure that the services they provide to the court are of a high standard in terms of the information provided, its presentation and the time scales which are set for this work to be completed.

Regulation 22
Sections 22 & 23

269.   Adoption agencies are required to write reports to the court in all freeing for adoption and adoption applications. They must do this within a period which is specified in the timetable drawn up by the court. Local authorities also have a duty to prepare a similar report when they receive notice of a proposed adoption when that adoption is not an agency one.

270.   Petitions may be lodged either in the Sheriff Court of the Sheriffdom within which the child is living or in the Court of Session. Applications to the Court of Session are rare and are usually made only in complicated cases. The court rules relating to the Court of Session are different from those in the Sheriff Court. In such cases it may be necessary to seek legal advice to ensure that the report meets the necessary requirements.

271.   Agencies should ensure that adequate preparation and training is given to social workers to equip them for providing this service. They should have access to the Regulations, court rules and primary legislation. They should be provided with training on the court process and presentation of evidence as it should not be assumed that all social workers have the necessary skills to do this. Such training should aim to improve social workers' confidence in appearing in court as witnesses.

Reports by a local authority or by an adoption agency

Regulation 22(1)

272.   The court rules specify the content of the report in applications for adoption orders or freeing for adoption orders and social workers should familiarise themselves with the court rules and the court's timetable for writing reports for the court. The report should fully address all the matters outlined in the court rules, the information on the background and circumstances of the child, his or her family, and where applicable the prospective adopters which has been discovered in the process of implementing the Regulations and any other matters which will assist the sheriff in reaching a decision. The report should consider whether adoption will safeguard and promote the welfare of the child throughout his or her life, should comment on and have regard to the views of the child, taking account of his or her age and maturity, and should have regard to his or her race, religion, language and culture.

Section 22

If the placing of the child was not an agency placement, the report should state whether or not the child was illegally placed with adopters. Each agency should ensure that reports are produced on time, using a format which meets the legal requirements.

Section 6A

273.   The consideration given to alternatives to adoption should be outlined. Where it is intended that contact will continue between the child and one or both of his or her birth parents, the reasons why adoption is preferred over other alternative courses of action should be specified. Where the children's hearing have given advice on the application, this advice must be provided to the court.

Regulation 22(2)

The Court Process

274.   In either a freeing for adoption or an adoption application, the sheriff will appoint a curator ad litem and a reporting officer. The reporting officer may be appointed prior to the lodging of a petition. The circumstances in which this might occur are where, for instance, everyone is ready to proceed but documents are awaited from overseas. The curator ad litem and the reporting officer will often be the same person unless the sheriff considers it inappropriate in the circumstances of the case.

Where a child has been freed for adoption, and an application has been made to adopt the child, a reporting officer will only be appointed if the child is twelve years or over, in order to witness his or her consent. The curator ad litem will be responsible for, amongst other matters, ascertaining whether the child wishes to express a view about the adoption and, if so, what his or her view is. This information may be given orally to the sheriff. The Rules of Court give further information on the duties of reporters and curators ad litem.

275.   At the hearing, once the sheriff has heard the evidence and read the reports he or she will decide, depending on the type of application, whether or not to grant a freeing for adoption order or an adoption order. Although very rarely used, the sheriff does have the powers in an adoption application which is not an adoption agency placement, to make an interim adoption order for a probationary period of up to two years. Where a sheriff decides not to grant a freeing for adoption order or an adoption order, the legal status of the child will remain as it was before the application was made, unless the sheriff decides to make another order, such as a section 11 (Children (Scotland) Act 1995) order.

ANNEX I

Issues that may be Addressed in the Home Study

The social worker should ensure that the following issues are addressed as appropriate in the home study

- the applicant's motivation in applying to be an adoptive parent and what he or she hopes to gain from a placement

- the applicant's understanding of adoption and the differences between adopting a child and being a birth parent

- the risks involved in placing a baby or young child whose birth parent comes from a group whose medical history or lifestyle would put the child at high medical risk, for instance the risk of contracting the AIDS virus, foetal alcohol syndrome or schizophrenia, or where there is little medical information available on one or both parents

- the potential for developmental delay in some children being placed and the possible difficulties of assessing the extent of the problem and its implications for the child's future

- information about the circumstances of children awaiting placement, the behavioural and emotional difficulties or the disabilities they may have and what types of difficulty or disability the applicant feels able to consider if any

- the effects of separation and loss on a child and how moving to a new placement may bring these back for the child

- the effects of physical and sexual abuse on children and the implications of caring for children who have been abused whether this is known at the time of placement or not

- the applicants' attitude towards birth parents and the circumstances which have led to their children being placed for adoption. This should include applicants' feelings about meeting the birth parents and about some degree of ongoing contact either with them or with wider family members

- the implications of a child being placed who is not legally secured

- the importance of being able to discuss the child's past with him or her, how they will talk to the child about adoption and his or her birth family and how they will help the child deal with the issues which this raises

- the family and life experience of the applicants

- the family and life experiences and attitudes towards adoption of any children of the applicant or any other members of the household

- the applicant's attitudes and values

- if there is a question of infertility, how the applicants have coped with this both individually and as a couple and how they came to a decision not to pursue treatment or further treatment or have dealt with the fact that there is not treatment available

- with a couple, what makes their relationship satisfying for them as well as any areas of friction. For single applicants, it will be necessary to discuss any relationships they have or may develop in future and the implications for any child placed

- special talents or relevant experience which the applicant has

- the applicant's experience of parenting his or her own children or caring for other people's children. This should include the steps he or she has taken to talk to his or her children about adoption

- the applicant's expectations of a child, including attitudes to education, health, food, hygiene and methods of control and discipline

- the applicant's attitude to working with the agency and to receiving post adoption support

- what support the applicant has, particularly from extended family and within the local neighbourhood or community

- the applicant's religion, degree of religious observance, and their capacity to care for a child of a different religion or from a more or less religious background than themselves

- the applicant's racial origin and cultural and linguistic background and any special experience and knowledge that may be shared with or have relevance to the care of a child of a particular racial origin or of mixed parentage or from a particular cultural background. These questions will be particularly relevant where applicants are hoping to adopt a child from overseas. Applicants should be informed of, and helped to understand, the agency's policies concerning how children's needs arising from racial origins and cultural and linguistic background can be met.

This is by no means an exhaustive list, and each home study will have a different emphasis. It should build up a picture of the applicant(s) and his or her family, what his or her strengths and weaknesses are and the kind of child he or she can best cope with.

ANNEX 2

Adoption or Freeing Applications

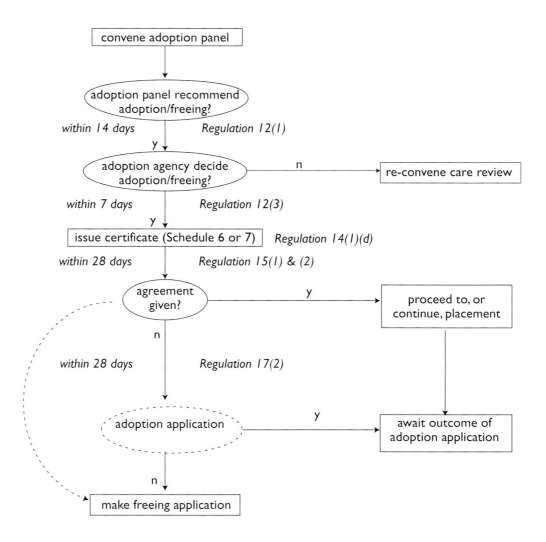

ANNEX 3

Adoption or Freeing Application where Child Subject to Supervision Requirement

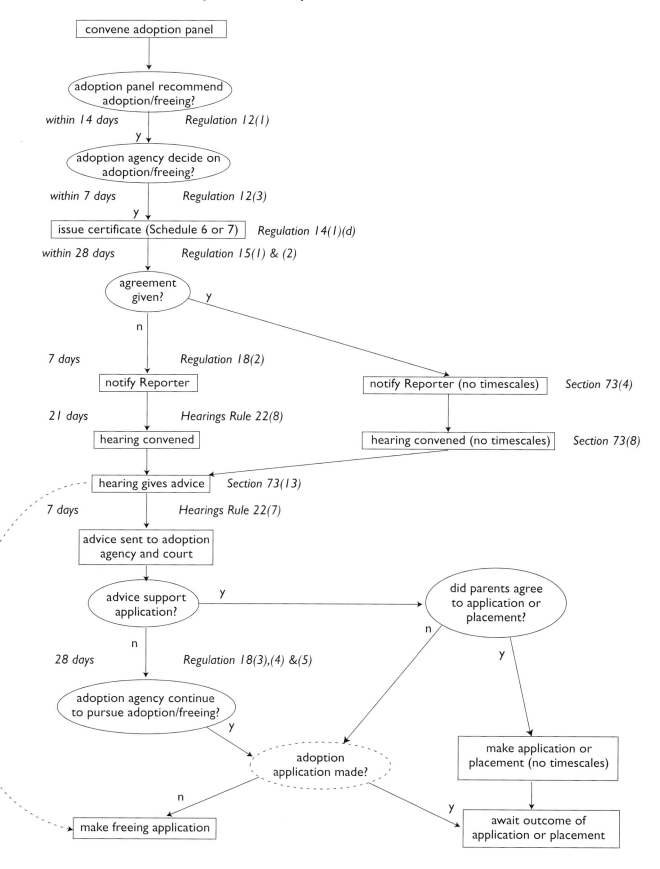

CHAPTER 2

Parental Responsibilities Orders

Introduction

Section 86 1.   The Act makes considerable changes in the form of and grounds for a local authority obtaining parental responsibilities for a child. The new parental responsibilities order granted by the court replaces the essentially administrative means for local authorities to obtain parental rights under the Social Work (Scotland) Act 1968. The change from "assumption and vesting of parental rights and powers" to a "parental responsibilities order" reflects the intention of the 1995 Act that parents or those undertaking the role of parent should have *responsibilities towards* as well as *rights over* children.

Section 11 2.   Under the Act anyone who claims an interest may in respect of a child apply for an order in relation to parental responsibilities or rights, or guardianship, etc., provided that person is not a local authority. This is distinct from a parental responsibility order which is the subject of this guidance. Records and reports should differentiate between an order under section 86 for parental responsibilities made in favour of a local authority and an order under section 11 made in favour of an individual.

Pre-application Action

3.   An application for a parental responsibilities order can be made whether or not a child is looked after by the local authority. Applications are likely to be unusual for a child who is not already looked after, but there could be appropriate cases, for instance, if a parent is dying of a terminal illness, is unable to identify anyone in the family network able or willing to care for the child after his or her death, and asks the local authority to apply for a parental responsibility order.

4.   Where a child is already looked after and it has been identified, within a child care review, that the child is in need of long-term care, security and stability away from his or her birth family, local authorities should consider, having sought the views of the child, whether a parental responsibilities order would be the best way to meet the child's needs and safeguard and promote his or her long-term welfare.

Section 16 5.   A court will only make a parental responsibilities order on the basis that the making of an order would be for the benefit of the child. Depriving a parent of his or her parental rights and responsibilities is a very serious step and a local authority should apply for an order only where it is clearly in the child's best interests. Whilst local authorities are not required by the Act to consider alternatives to a parental responsibilities order, it would be good practice to outline in an application to the court why a parental responsibilities order is considered the most beneficial outcome for the child and how it will be used. In reaching the decision whether or not to apply for an order local authorities should consider the following questions

- Where a child is away from home, is it clearly demonstrated and documented that restoration of the child to his or her parents or extended family is unlikely to be in the child's best interests, or has been tried and failed and further attempts are unlikely to be in the child's best interests?

  Section 25

- Where the child is accommodated, is accommodation unable to fulfil the child's immediate and long-term needs or can a long-term, and reliable, accommodation agreement be reached with the child's parents, which will mean that accommodation can continue to meet the child's needs?

- Where the child is subject to a supervision requirement, could variation of the conditions of the supervision requirement meet the child's immediate and long-term needs or does the need to attend a children's hearing at least annually mean that supervision creates needless instability and uncertainty for the child?

  Section 73

- If the long-term plan is for the child to remain with current foster carers, are the foster carers willing to apply for a residence order, and would this better meet the immediate and long-term needs of the child than the local authority applying for a parental responsibilities order? A residence order would give the foster carers parental responsibilities and rights which, depending on the nature of the order applied for, or obtained, might or might not be shared with a parent or someone else with parental responsibilities and rights. Where appropriate, the former foster carer could be paid a residence allowance.

  Section 11

  Schedule 4 para 26(3)

- Would the child's best interests be better met by adoption either by his or her current foster carers or in a new family?

- In the event of one or both parents being dead, is there anyone with an interest in the child who should be encouraged to apply to be the child's guardian? Would this meet the child's needs for someone to exercise parental responsibilities?

  Section 11(2)

6. The sheriff will, taking account of the age and maturity of the child concerned, give the child an opportunity to express his or her views if the child wishes to do so, about making an order and any conditions it is proposed be attached to the order, and will have regard to the views expressed by the child. A child aged twelve or more will be presumed to be of sufficient age and maturity to form a view but younger children, will also be given the opportunity to express a view if they have formed one, under Sheriff Court Rules. The local authority should discuss plans with the child, so that he or she can understand the effects of a parental responsibilities order, so far as can be expected at his or her age and maturity. Different methods of communication may be needed to help a child with a disability to express his or her views. The local authority will need to demonstrate to the court that an order is in the child's best interests whether or not this view is accepted by the child.

  Section 16

7. Local authorities should have regard, as far as is practicable, to needs arising from a child's racial, religious, cultural and linguistic background when they look after a child. Would the making of a parental responsibilities order positively or negatively affect the local authority's ability to meet his or her needs? If the effect is likely to be detrimental, for instance, because a parent has been the main source of religious or cultural knowledge for a child and it is intended to apply to reduce contact as part of the order, what alternative plans have been made to meet the child's needs?

  Section 17(4)

Section 17(3)   8.   As well as ascertaining the views of the child, before making any decision with respect to a child who they are looking after, the local authority is bound, so far as is reasonably practicable, to ascertain the views of the child's parents or any other person who is not a parent but who has parental rights in relation to the child or any other person whose views the authority consider to be relevant. Given the far reaching nature and effect of the decision to be made, the authority should make serious and substantial efforts to ascertain the views of the above people. This could mean advertising for a missing parent or visiting any known relatives or friends to see if the parents' whereabouts are known to them. Any search should be within a timescale which is consistent with the welfare of the child. Parents and others who have parental rights may be opposed to the making of a parental responsibilities order in favour of the local authority. Their views should be carefully listened to and any suggested alternatives to the order should be evaluated. This should not necessarily deter an application which should be based on the best interests of the child.

9.   In order for a local authority to obtain a parental responsibilities order, it will be necessary that each parent or person with parental rights in relation to the child either agrees or consents to the order or that the sheriff dispenses with the consent of each of these people.

10.   Decisions to apply for parental responsibilities orders should be made by a designated senior officer within the local authority and informed by legal advice. Full consideration should be given to any question of an application for a parental responsibilities order at the statutory care review. Where the conclusion of the review is that a parental responsibilities order will meet the child's best interests, a recommendation to this effect should be made to the designated officer. Where a child is not looked after by the local authority, the recommendation to apply for a parental responsibilities order should be made at a planning meeting. Some authorities may choose to widen the remit of their adoption panel to include consideration of plans for all children in need of permanent placement away from their birth families. In that event adoption panels would advise on recommendations concerning applications for parental responsibilities orders.

Requirements for Making an Order

Section 16   11.   The paramount consideration of the court in considering an application for a parental responsibilities order, is the welfare of the child throughout his or her childhood. In considering the child's welfare, the court must take into account any views expressed by the child. The court will not make an order unless it would be better for the child than not making an order.

Section 86(2)   12.   Additionally, the court must be satisfied either that each relevant person that is, a parent of the child or person who for the time being has parental rights in relation to the child

- freely, and with full understanding of what is involved, agrees unconditionally to the making of the order.

or
- is a person who

    is not known, cannot be found or is incapable of giving agreement

    is withholding such agreement unreasonably

has persistently failed, without reasonable cause to fulfil one of the parental responsibilities to safeguard and promote the child's health, development and welfare; or to maintain personal relations and direct contact with the child on a regular basis

has seriously ill-treated the child and because of that serious ill-treatment or for some other reason, the reintegration of the child into that person's household is unlikely.

Where a relevant person agrees unconditionally to the making of the Order, his or her agreement will be witnessed by the reporting officer appointed by the court.

13.   No time span is prescribed over which children must be looked after before a local authority can apply for a parental responsibilites order. The criteria for dispensing with agreement are different from the criteria under the 1968 Act for assuming and vesting parental rights and powers and are the same as those for dispensing with agreement to adoption.

Conditions on the Order

14.   The sheriff may impose any conditions to the parental responsibilities order which he or she considers appropriate. Such conditions can be varied or discharged by the sheriff on the application of the child, the local authority, anyone who immediately before the making of the order was a relevant person, (either a parent of the child or a person who, for the time being, has parental rights in relation to the child) or any other person claiming an interest.

Section 86(5)

Section 86(4)

15.   Except where the court restricts or terminates contact children who are subject to a parental responsibilities order must be allowed reasonable contact with anyone who, prior to the parental responsibilities order being made, was a relevant person, or who had a residence or contact order in force in respect of the child or who was entitled to have the child residing with him or her under an Order made by a court of competent jurisdiction. Where possible, appropriate arrangements for the child to have reasonable contact with those people should be agreed with them by the local authority without the need for recourse to a court order.

Section 88

16.   The sheriff can however, make an Order which specifies, restricts or terminates contact between the child and any of the people specified above or any other person. This will either be the result of an application by the local authority, the child, or any person with an interest or because the sheriff has decided at some time while the order is in force to specify, restrict or terminate contact, even though no-one has made an application. The sheriff can attach any conditions to the contact order he or she considers appropriate. The sheriff may vary or discharge a contact order on the application of the child, the local authority or any person with an interest. The discharge or termination of a parental responsibilities order also terminates the contact order.

Making the Application

17.   An application for a parental responsibilities order should be made on a form prescribed under the Sheriff Court Rules. Once the application is made the sheriff will appoint a reporting officer and a curator ad litem. If the sheriff considers it appropriate, these two appointments can be held by the same person. The sheriff

may appoint a reporting officer prior to the application being made for example where the local authority is awaiting receipt of documents from abroad before making an application. A request for such an appointment must be made in writing to the sheriff clerk, specifying the reasons.

18.   The reporting officer and the curator ad litem must report in writing within four weeks or within any other period of time specified by the sheriff. The main duties of the reporting officer are to

- witness any agreements to the parental responsibilities order, made by relevant people who are within the United Kingdom
- ascertain whether each relevant person, who can be found, understands the implications and effects of a parental responsibilities order and is aware that he or she can apply to a sheriff for a variation or revocation of the order
- ascertain whether there is any other person, apart from those mentioned in the application, upon whom notice of the application should be served.

The role of the curator ad litem is to

- safeguard the interests of the child who is subject of the application and ensure that the welfare of the child is paramount
- ascertain whether the facts stated in the application are correct except where investigation of the facts falls within the duties of the reporting officer
- ascertain from the child whether he or she wishes to express a view and where the child does, ascertain his or her view. The view of the child may be conveyed to the sheriff orally by the curator ad litem. (The sheriff may order "such procedural steps to be taken as he considers appropriate" to ascertain the views of the child. The sheriff must not make a parental responsibilites order unless an opportunity for the child's views to be obtained or heard has been given. The sheriff may make directions about the confidentiality of the views of the child.)
- ascertain whether a parental responsibilities order would safeguard and promote the welfare of the child
- report on the current circumstances and care of the child.

19.   Once the reports are received, the sheriff will order a diet of the hearing to be fixed. Anyone whose agreement to the order is required or must be dispensed with, and anyone claiming to be the father of the child, even if he does not have parental rights and responsibilities, provided their whereabouts are known, must be informed of the proceedings by the local authority. If any of these people appear, they are entitled to be heard by the court. All evidence will be given in their presence or in the presence of their solicitor. If they do not appear, an order may still be made by the sheriff in their absence. Before making an order, the sheriff must consider all the reports which have been submitted. The sheriff will then either grant an order or refuse the application. Where an order is granted it may contain any conditions the sheriff thinks appropriate.

Referral to a Children's Hearing

Section 73(4)   20.   If a child, for whom it is intended to apply for a parental responsibilities order is subject to a supervision requirement, the case must be referred to the Principal

Reporter prior to making the application. The children's hearing is required to consider the case and within seven days send a report to the court, the local authority, the child, any relevant person and any safeguarder appointed in the proceedings outlining its advice on the appropriateness of the order.

21. Where the children's hearing reports that it is not in favour of the making of a parental responsibilities order, the local authority should take this advice into consideration before deciding whether to proceed with an application.

Local Authority Responsibilities under an Order

22. The local authority, when it obtains a parental responsibilities order, obtains all parental rights and responsibilities towards the child, except the right to agree, or decline to agree, to the child being freed for adoption or adopted.

Section 86(3)

23. The local authority has a duty to fulfil the following parental responsibilities

Section 1

- to safeguard and promote the child's health, development and welfare

- to provide in a manner appropriate to the stage of development of the child, direction or guidance to the child

- to maintain personal relations and direct contact with the child on a regular basis

- to act as the child's legal representative, (but only insofar as the child is not able to exercise the right, because of lack of maturity, or does not choose to exercise the right (Age of Legal Capacity (Scotland) Act 1991));

so far as compliance is practicable and in the interests of the child. The above responsibilities apply until the child reaches the age of sixteen years, except the responsibility to provide guidance which exists until the child reaches eighteen years. The local authority has the parental rights under section 2 of the Act, including the right to regulate where the child lives, in order to help him or her fulfil the above responsibilities.

24. The order has the effect of making the child looked after by the local authority, if he or she is not already looked after, and the local authority will, therefore, have duties towards the child as well as rights and responsibilities. These are explained in Volume 2 of the guidance on the Act which covers children who are looked after.

Section 17

25. The local authority may place the child with a parent, guardian, relative or friend, either for a fixed period or until they decide to end the arrangement, if it is considered this would benefit the child. Prior to allowing the child to live with a parent or guardian, the local authority should consider whether any checks or references are needed in order to safeguard the child's welfare. If a child is placed with a relative or friend, this placement will be subject to the Fostering of Children (Scotland) Regulations 1996. Where a local authority allows a child to live with a parent, guardian, relative or friend the local authority still retains all parental rights and responsibilities. The parent, guardian, relative or friend has the responsibility to do "what is reasonable in all the circumstances to safeguard the child's health, development and welfare". Where a child is placed at home with a parent this will generally be because the child or parent's circumstances have changed since the order was made and with a view to the parent resuming full care of the child and

Section 87

the order being revoked. In most circumstances, the local authority should amend the care plan with the parents and the child so that, increasingly, normal parental tasks and decision-making are restored to the parents. Statutory review provisions apply to children subject to parental responsibilities orders placed with parents, guardians, relatives or friends.

Section 87(3)   26.   If the local authority has placed the child with a parent, guardian, relative or friend and wishes to end the arrangement, they must give notice in writing to the person telling them to return the child on a certain date. This notice must either be delivered by hand or sent by recorded delivery. It is an offence for a parent, guardian, relative or friend not to comply with this notice. If it proves necessary to remove a child in an emergency, notice may be given simultaneously with the removal of the child.

Section 87(3)   27.   It is not possible for a parental responsibilities order to be transferred from one local authority to another. If the child moves such a distance that proper support of the child is not possible, then an agreement will need to be made for the local authority, where the child is living, to supervise the case on behalf of the local authority which obtained the order.

Variation, Discharge or Termination of the Order

Section 86(5)   28.   The sheriff may vary or discharge a parental responsibilities order on the application of a child, any person who immediately before the making of the order was a relevant person or who claims an interest, or the local authority. The application will be by way of a minute and the information required by the court is outlined in the Sheriff Court Rules. The sheriff may appoint a curator ad litem.

29.   Whilst parental responsibilities orders will normally be obtained in order to safeguard the long-term welfare of a child, circumstances may change for the child. The plan for the child may not work out as intended or one or both of the parents or other relevant persons may have a change in their circumstances. Where circumstances have changed, consideration should be given at the child care review as to whether the order is still in the best interests of the child and, if not, whether an application should be made to discharge the parental responsibilities order or vary any of the conditions. The local authority should seek the child's views before reaching a decision.

30.   Even though the local authority concludes that a parental responsibilities order should remain in force or that it does not need to be varied, the child may hold a different view. In these circumstances, the child should be helped to contact a solicitor if he or she wishes to apply for a variation or discharge of the order.

31.   If a parental responsibilities order has not been discharged, then it will automatically terminate

- on the child's eighteenth birthday

- when the child is freed for adoption or adopted

- if an order is made for his or her return under Part 1 of the Child Abduction and Custody Act 1985 or a decision, other than a decision relating to rights of access (section 25(2) of the 1985 Act) is registered with respect to him or her under section 16 of that Act.

The making of a residence order will not automatically terminate a parental responsibilities order. The petitioner will need to petition the court for both a residence order and the simultaneous discharge of the parental responsibilities order.

Offences in Relation to Parental Responsibilities Orders

32.   Any person who knowingly or without lawful authority or reasonable excuse, with regard to a child, in respect of whom a parental responsibilites order has been made

- fails to comply with a notice requiring him or her to return a child (See paragraph 26 above)   *Section 89*

- harbours or conceals a child who has run away, or been taken away, or whose return is required (except where this is in a short-term refuge provided under section 38 of the Act)

- induces, assists, or incites a child to run away or stay away or takes the child away from the placement where he or she is looked after

is guilty of an offence. He or she is liable, on summary conviction, to a fine not exceeding level 5 on the standard scale or imprisonment for no more than six months or both.

Regulations and Direction

STATUTORY INSTRUMENTS

1996 No. 3266 (S. 254)

CHILDREN AND YOUNG PERSONS

The Adoption Agencies
(Scotland) Regulations 1996

Made	*24th December 1996*
Laid before Parliament	*31st December 1996*
Coming into force	*1st April 1997*

ARRANGEMENT OF REGULATIONS

Schedule 1 – Information in application for approval to act or continue to act as an adoption society for a specific service

Schedule 2 – Particulars of parties to adoption

Schedule 3 – Form of reference by adoption agency to Principal Reporter for advice by children's hearing to the court

Schedule 4 – Memorandum - adoption of children

Schedule 5 – Memorandum - freeing of children for adoption

Schedule 6 – Parent's agreement in respect of placement of child for adoption

Schedule 7 – Parent's agreement in respect of the making of an application to free a child for adoption

The Secretary of State, in exercise of the powers conferred on him by sections 3(1A), 9 and 27(2) of the Adoption (Scotland) Act 1978(a) and of all other powers enabling him in that behalf, hereby makes the following Regulations:

Citation, commencement and extent

1.   (1) These Regulations may be cited as the Adoption Agencies (Scotland) Regulations 1996 and shall come into force on 1st April 1997.

(2) These Regulations shall apply to Scotland only.

Interpretation

2.   (1) In these Regulations, unless the context otherwise requires—
   "the Act" means the Adoption (Scotland) Act 1978;

   "the 1995 Act" means the Children (Scotland) Act 1995(b);

   "adoption agency" means a local authority or an approved adoption society within the meaning of the Act;

   "adoption panel" means a panel appointed in accordance with regulation 7;

   "court" means an authorised court as defined by section 56 of the Act;

   "health board" means a health board constituted under section 2 of the National Health Service (Scotland) Act 1978(c);

   "parent" has the meaning given to that term in section 65 of the Act(d).

(2) In these Regulations any reference to an adoption order shall include reference to an order under section 49 of the Act and any reference to a person proposing to adopt a child shall include reference to a person proposing to apply for such an order.

(3) In these Regulations any reference to a numbered regulation or schedule shall be construed as a reference to the regulation or schedule bearing that number in these Regulations, and any reference to a numbered paragraph shall be a reference to the paragraph bearing that number in the regulation in which the reference to the numbered paragraph is made.

Approved adoption societies

3.   (1) An application to the Secretary of State under section 3 of the Act for approval as an adoption society shall—

   (a) be made in writing;

   (b) provide information about the applicant as to the matters specified in sub-sections (3) to (5) of that section; and

---

(a)1978 c.28; section 3(1A) of the 1978 Act substituted by section 94 (brought into force for regulation making purposes by the Children (Scotland) Act 1995 Commencement No. 3 Order 1996 S.I. 1996/3201) of the Children (Scotland) Act 1995 (c.36) ('the 1995 Act"); in section 9 subsection (2) was amended by paragraph 5(a) and subsection (3A) was inserted by paragraph 5(b), of Schedule 2 to the 1995 Act; and section 27(2) was substituted by paragraph 19 of Schedule 2 to the 1995 Act.

(b)1995 c.36.

(c)1978 c.29.

(d)Section 65 was amended by the 1995 Act, Schedule 2, paragraph 29.

(c) where the application is for approval to act or continue to act as an adoption society functioning in relation to some service maintained, or to be maintained, as part of the Scottish Adoption Service, specify that service and provide further information about the applicant as to the matters specified in Schedule 1.

(2) An unincorporated body is prohibited from applying to the Secretary of State for his approval under section 3 of the Act to its acting as an adoption society.

(3) An approved adoption society shall notify the Secretary of State in writing of any change in its name or in the address of its registered or head office within one month after such change.

(4) An approved adoption society shall prepare an annual report on the exercise of its functions in relation to adoption and shall provide the Secretary of State with a copy of such a report as soon as possible after the expiry of the year to which the report relates.

(5) As soon as possible after the end of each financial year of an approved adoption society, the society shall provide the Secretary of State with an abstract of the society's accounts for that year, signed on behalf of the society and certified by its auditors.

Complaints procedure of approved adoption societies

4. (1) The procedures established by an approved adoption society for the purpose of dealing with complaints arising in relation to the exercise of its functions shall comply with paragraphs (2) to (8) hereinafter known as the "complaints procedure".

(2) The complaints procedure shall apply to any representations (including complaints) received by the approved adoption society in writing from—

(a) any person, or anyone acting on behalf of a person;

(b) a child or, on behalf of a child, any person with parental responsibilities or parental rights in respect of the child; or

(c) any person with an interest in the child and in the functions of the society in relation to the child,

where the representations relate to the society's exercise, or failure or refusal to exercise, in respect of that person or child any of the functions for which the society is approved under section 3 of the Act.

(3) The complaints procedure shall provide for the appointment of—

(a) one of the employees of the approved adoption society for the purpose of receiving, and acknowledging as soon as reasonably practicable, any representations under the procedure, arranging for the consideration of them and for the giving of a response to them on behalf of the society; and

(b) one or more persons for the purpose of investigating the representations, each being a person who is not a member or employee of the society, or related or married to, or living with such a member or employee.

(4) The complaints procedure shall provide for—

(a) a response in writing by the adoption society to the substance of the representations to be given to the person who made them, as soon as reasonably practicable following receipt of the representations by the society;

(b) arrangements to be made by the society to appoint a complaints review committee for the purpose of considering further representations, where within 28 days from giving a response under sub-paragraph (a), the society receives notice in writing from the person who made the representations that he is not satisfied with the response;

(c) any complaints review committee appointed by the society to be composed of 3 persons, at least one of whom shall be a person who is not a member or employee of the society and is not related or married to, or living with such a member or employee, and none of whom shall be a person appointed by the society for the purpose mentioned in sub-paragraph (3)(b);

(d) the complaints review committee to consider the representations as soon as reasonably practicable, and to report to the society in writing with a recommendation on the disposal of the matter along with reasons for that recommendation; and

(e) the society, as soon as reasonably practicable, to take a decision on the matter after it has received the report from the complaints review committee, taking account of the recommendation of that committee, and to give notice in writing of that decision, with the reasons for it, to the person who made the representations.

(5) An approved adoption society shall keep a record of—

(a) any representations received under the complaints procedure;

(b) the investigation into any such representations, including the report of any complaints review committee appointed under sub-paragraph (4)(b); and

(c) the disposal of the representations.

(6) An approved adoption society shall make available information about its complaints procedure to—

(a) any person having an interest and who requests it; and

(b) every person in respect of whom the society exercises, or decides not to exercise, any of the functions for which it is approved under section 3 of the Act.

(7) An approved adoption society may make arrangements to deal with any informal representations received by it from any person in relation to the exercise, or failure or refusal to exercise, any of the functions for which it is approved under section 3 of the Act, provided that—

(a) when replying to any informal representations the society advises the person who made them of the entitlement to make representations under the complaints procedure; and

(b) the society provides that person with such assistance as is appropriate and as he may require in making representations under the complaints procedure should he wish to do so.

(8) An approved adoption society shall take such steps as are appropriate to ensure that the employees of the society are aware of its complaints procedure.

Cessation as approved adoption society

5. (1) An approved adoption society which intends to cease to act as an adoption society shall notify the Secretary of State in writing of such intention at least 3 months before the intended date of such cessation.

(2) An approved adoption society which has ceased to act as an adoption society shall notify the Secretary of State in writing that it has ceased so to act, as soon thereafter as is reasonably practicable.

Appointment of medical and legal advisers

6. (1) An adoption agency shall appoint such number of registered medical practitioners as it considers necessary for the purpose of providing it with medical advice in connection with the exercise of its functions.

(2) An adoption agency shall appoint such number of solicitors or advocates as it considers necessary for the purpose of providing it with legal advice in connection with the exercise of its functions and for the purpose of this paragraph "solicitor" means a person qualified to practise as a solicitor further to the provisions of section 4 of the Solicitors (Scotland) Act 1980(a); and "advocate" means a practising member of the Faculty of Advocates.

Appointment, composition, qualifications etc. of adoption panels

7. (1) A local authority shall appoint an adoption panel for the purpose of considering and advising on the matters specified in regulation 11 and may appoint such additional adoption panels as it considers necessary.

(a)1980c.46.

(2) An approved adoption society which is carrying out or proposing to carry out functions described in regulation 11 shall appoint an adoption panel for the purpose of considering and advising on the matters specified in that regulation, and may appoint such additional adoption panels as it considers necessary.

(3) An adoption agency shall satisfy itself that the numbers, qualifications and experience of individual members of an adoption panel will enable it effectively to discharge its functions under regulation 11.

(4) An adoption panel shall consist of not less than 6 persons each of whom shall be competent to assess whether any recommendation in relation to a child to be made by virtue of regulation 11(1) is likely to promote the welfare of the child, and shall include at least one man and at least one woman.

(5) The persons appointed to an adoption panel shall include—

    (a) a person appointed as a medical adviser to the adoption agency under regulation 6(1); and

    (b) a person appointed as a legal adviser to the adoption agency under regulation 6(2).

(6) An adoption panel shall make the recommendations specified—

    (a) in regulation 11 only when at least 3 of its members, excluding any medical and legal adviser appointed to the panel under paragraph (5), meet as a panel; and

    (b) in regulation 11(1) (a) only when a legal adviser appointed to the adoption panel under paragraph (5) is present, or legal advice has been provided to the panel by such an adviser.

Duties of adoption agencies in making arrangements for freeing for adoption

8.   An adoption agency which is a local authority shall not make application for an order under section 18 of the Act (freeing a child for adoption) unless—

    (a) the adoption agency has, so far as is reasonably practicable, ascertained the particulars set out in Part I of Schedule 2;

    (b) the adoption agency has obtained a report prepared within the previous 12 months by a fully registered medical practitioner as to the health of the child;

    (c) the adoption agency has prepared a written report containing its observations on the matters referred to in this regulation and has passed that report, together with all information obtained by it by virtue of this regulation, to the adoption panel or to another adoption agency; and

    (d) the adoption agency, after considering all the information obtained in pursuance of this regulation and having regard to the recommendation of the adoption panel under regulation 11 and all other circumstances, has concluded in accordance with sections 6 and 6A of the Act that adoption is likely to best meet the needs of the child, and that either—

        (i) regulations 17(2), or regulation 18(3) or (5) apply to the case of the child; or

        (ii) the welfare of the child would be best met by the making of an application for an order under section 18 of the Act at that time whether or not the child has been placed with a person with a view to his being adopted by that person.

Duties of adoption agencies in making arrangements for adoption

9.   (1) An adoption agency shall not place or secure the placing of a child in the care and possession of any person proposing to adopt the child until—

    (a) the adoption agency has so far as is reasonably practicable, ascertained the particulars set out in Schedule 2;

    (b) the adoption agency has obtained a report prepared within the previous 12 months by a fully registered medical practitioner as to the health of the child;

(c) the adoption agency has obtained a report prepared within the previous 12 months by a fully registered medical practitioner as to the health of each person proposing to adopt the child;

(d) that person has been interviewed by or on behalf of the adoption agency;

(e) the adoption agency has satisfied itself by a visit on its behalf that any premises in Great Britain within which that person intends that the child shall have his home are satisfactory;

(f) the adoption agency has made enquiries to satisfy itself that there is no reason to believe that it would be detrimental to the welfare of the child for him to be kept by that person and by that person in those premises and has inquired of every local authority in whose area those premises are situated whether that local authority has reason to believe that it would be detrimental to the welfare of the child—

    (i) for him to be kept by that person in those premises; or

    (ii) for the proposed adoption to proceed;

(g) the adoption agency has prepared a written report containing its observations on the matters referred to in this regulation and has passed that report, together with all information obtained by it by virtue of this regulation, to the adoption panel or to another adoption agency;

(h) the adoption agency has concluded in accordance with section 6 and 6A of the Act that the welfare of the child would be best met by his being so placed.

(2) The adoption agency shall arrange such medical investigations and tests as are considered necessary to be carried out on the child and shall arrange that a report based thereon is obtained from a fully registered medical practitioner unless such tests have already been carried out and the findings are known to the agency.

(3) Wherever practicable any report in connection with paragraph (2) shall be included in the report obtained by the adoption agency under paragraph l(b) of this regulation.

Duties of adoption agencies in assessing prospective adopters

10. (1) An adoption agency shall prepare and make available to any person with an interest a statement of the general criteria which the agency applies for the purpose of considering whether any person may be accepted by the agency for assessment as an adoptive parent.

(2) An adoption agency shall from time to time review the general criteria prepared by it under paragraph (1).

(3) In considering any application by a person to be assessed by the adoption agency as an adoptive parent, the agency shall apply the general criteria prepared under paragraph (1), and undertake any further steps necessary to consider the application.

(4) Where following any action mentioned in paragraph (3) the adoption agency decides—

(a) that the person should not be accepted for assessment as an adoptive parent, the agency shall give notice in writing to that person; or

(b) that the person should be accepted for assessment as mentioned, the agency shall assess the case and refer it to the adoption panel for a recommendation to the agency on the matter.

(5) Where referring the case of a prospective adopter to the adoption panel under paragraph (4), the adoption agency shall at the same time give—

(a) a copy of the report on the case to the adoption panel; and

(b) notice to the prospective adopter that the case has been referred to the adoption panel and a copy of the report provided to the panel, (excluding any information from third parties given in confidence).

Functions of adoption panels

11. (1) Subject to paragraphs (4), (5) and (6), an adoption panel shall consider the case of every child and proposed placement referred to it by the adoption agency and the case of

every prospective adopter referred to it by the agency under regulation 10(4), and shall make recommendations to the agency on such of the following matters as may be appropriate—

   (a) whether adoption is in the best interests of a child and if the panel recommends that it is whether an application under section 18 of the Act should be made to free the child for adoption;

   (b) whether a prospective adopter is suitable to be an adoptive parent; and

   (c) whether a prospective adopter would be a suitable adoptive parent for a particular child.

(2) Where making a recommendation to the adoption agency under paragraph (1)(a) whether adoption is in the best interests of the child—

   (a) an adoption panel shall provide a written report of the consideration given by it to the alternatives to adoption before coming to that recommendation; and

   (b) the adoption panel shall, when recommending in addition that following any adoption there be continued contact between the child and one or both of his then parents, provide a written report of the reasons why adoption is recommended rather than an alternative course of action.

(3) An adoption panel may make the recommendation specified in paragraph (1)(b) only where they had the opportunity to meet with the prospective adopter and had the opportunity to discuss the matter with him.

(4) An adoption panel may make the recommendations specified in paragraph (1) at the same time or at different times but it shall make the recommendation specified in paragraph (1)(c) in respect of a particular child and prospective adopter only if—

   (a) at the meeting of the panel at which that recommendation is to be made a recommendation is also made that adoption is in the best interests of the child; or

   (b) an adoption agency decision has been made in accordance with regulation 12(1) that adoption is in the best interests of the child; and

   (c) in either case—

      (i) at the meeting of the panel at which the recommendation specified in paragraph (1)(c) is to be made a recommendation is also made that the prospective adopter is suitable to be an adoptive parent; or

     (ii) an adoption agency decision has been made in accordance with regulation 12(1) that the prospective adopter is suitable to be an adoptive parent.

(5) In considering what recommendations to make the panel shall have regard to the duties imposed upon the adoption agency by sections 6, 6A and 7 of the Act (duty to promote welfare of child, consider alternatives to adoption and religious upbringing of adopted child) and shall as the case may be—

   (a) consider and take into account all the information and reports passed to it by virtue of regulation 8(c) or 9(1)(g) and in accordance with paragraph (6);

   (b) request the adoption agency to obtain any other relevant information which the panel considers necessary;

   (c) obtain legal advice in relation to each case.

(6) An adoption agency may request an adoption panel to consider and advise on any other matters relevant to the agency's performance of its functions under the Act, or under these regulations or under any other regulations made under the Act.

Adoption agency decisions and notifications

12. (1) An adoption agency shall make a decision within 14 days from the date of the recommendation of the adoption panel, on a matter referred to in regulations 11(1)(a), (b) or (c) and only after taking into account the relevant recommendation of that adoption panel.

(2) An adoption agency shall record in writing its reasons for any decision under paragraph (1) which is contrary to a recommendation of the adoption panel.

(3) Within 7 days from the date of a decision under paragraph (1) the adoption agency shall, as appropriate, notify in writing—

   (a) the parents of the child, including where the adoption agency considers this to be in the child's interests, the father or mother of a child who is a parent in terms of section 15(1) of the 1995 Act but does not have parental responsibilities, or the guardian of the child if their whereabouts are known to the adoption agency, of its decision as to whether it considers adoption to be in the best interests of the child;

   (b) the persons to be notified under sub-paragraph (a) of its decision as to whether an application under section 18 of the Act should be made to free the child for adoption;

   (c) the prospective adopter of its decision as to whether it considers him to be suitable to be an adoptive parent; and

   (d) the prospective adopter of its decision as to whether he would be suitable as such for a particular child.

(4) As soon as is reasonably practicable after making a decision under paragraph (1) that adoption is not likely to best meet the needs of the child as there is some better, practicable alternative, or that an application under section 18 of the Act would be in the child's best interests, or after deciding that the agreement mentioned in regulation 14(1)(d) is not forthcoming, an approved adoption society shall take such steps, if any, in relation to the case as they consider appropriate and in the interests of the child.

(5) A local authority referring the case of a child subject to a supervision requirement to the Principal Reporter under section 73(4)(c)(ii) or (iii) of the 1995 Act or section 22A of the Act shall not do so until it is in a position to proceed under regulation 15(1) or 15(2), and shall do so in the form set out in Schedule 3 or in form to like effect.

Freeing or placing for adoption a child subject to a supervision requirement

13. (1) An adoption agency which is a local authority shall, for the purpose of considering whether it is satisfied in accordance with section 73(4)(c)(ii) or (iii) of the 1995 Act that the best interests of a child subject to a supervision requirement would be served by their applying under section 18 of the Act for an order freeing the child for adoption or placing the child for adoption, take into account a recommendation of the adoption panel on the matter under regulation 11(1) before coming to a decision.

(2) An approved adoption society shall, for the purpose of considering whether it is satisfied in accordance with section 22A of the Act that the best interests of a child subject to a supervision requirement would be served by its placing the child for adoption, take into account a recommendation of the adoption panel on the matter under regulation 11(1) before coming to a decision.

Information and certificate for parents on notification of adoption agency's decision

14. (1) The adoption agency shall, when notifying the parents or guardian of a child of the agency's decision under regulation 12 on a matter referred to in regulation 11(1)(a)-

   (a) shall provide each parent or guardian with a memorandum either—

      (i) in the form set out in Schedule 4 where it is proposed to make arrangements for adoption of the child; or—

      (ii) in the form set out in Schedule 5 where it is proposed to make an application for a freeing order under section 18 of the Act;

   (b) shall take such steps as are reasonably practicable to ensure that each parent or guardian signs and returns to the agency a certificate in the form set out in Schedule 4 or 5 as the case may be, or a form to the like effect, certifying that he has read and understood that memorandum;

   (c) shall at the request of the parents or guardian provide them with the names and addresses of adoption agencies, if they are available, which might meet their wishes regarding the child's upbringing in a particular religious persuasion;

(d) at the same time provide each parent or guardian with a certificate in the form set out in Schedule 6 or 7 as the case may be, certifying the agreement or otherwise of the parent or guardian with the proposal under paragraph (1)(a)(i) or, as the case may be, (ii); and

(e) ensure, so far as reasonably practicable, that each parent or guardian completes and signs the certificate and returns it to the agency within 28 days.

(2) Where the identity of a parent as defined by section 15(1) of the 1995 Act but not having parental responsibilities of a child is known to the adoption agency, it shall so far as it considers it reasonably practicable and in the interests of the child—

(a) carry out in respect of such parent the requirements of paragraph (1)(a) and (b), as if they applied to him, unless the agency is satisfied that another adoption agency has so complied with those requirements;

(b) obtain in respect of such parent the information required under Schedule 2 and ascertain so far as possible whether he intends to apply for any parental responsibilities or parental rights in relation to the child, or enter into a parental responsibilities agreement under section 4 of the 1995 Act.

Return of consent certificate

15. (1) Where each parent or guardian within a period of 28 days from the date of receipt of the certificate mentioned in regulation 14(1)(d) returns to the adoption agency the certificate specified in regulation 14 stating his agreement to the agency's decision, the agency shall determine that such agreement as is mentioned in section 16(1)(b)(i) or, as the case may be, section 18(1)(a) of the Act is likely to be forthcoming and for the purposes of section 27(1) of the Act the certificate shall be sufficient proof of consent.

(2) Unless the agency receives the certificate referred to in paragraph (1) within the 28 days specified (or where the parent or guardian cannot be contacted within 28 days from reasonable efforts being made to make contact), the agency shall proceed as though such agreement mentioned in paragraph (1) is unlikely to be forthcoming.

(3) Where a parent or guardian who has returned a certificate under regulation 15(1) subsequently notifies in writing to an agency that his agreement is no longer forthcoming, the agency shall from the date of receipt of the notification proceed, for the purposes of paragraph (1) but not where the child has already been placed for adoption for the purposes of section 27(1) of the Act, as though such agreement under the Act as is referred to in paragraph (1) is unlikely to be forthcoming and shall, if the adoption agency is a local authority, perform the duties referred to in regulation 17, or as the case may be regulation 18, as appropriate in light of the change of circumstances.

Appropriate steps as soon as practicable by adoption society

16. As soon as is reasonably practicable after making a decision to proceed under regulation 15(2) as though the agreement is unlikely to be forthcoming, or from the date of receipt of a notification under regulation 15(3), an approved adoption society shall take such steps, if any, in relation to the case as they consider appropriate and in the interests of the child.

Legal process where the child is not subject to supervision requirement

17. (1) This regulation applies where a child is not subject to a supervision requirement and arrangements for adoption are proposed in respect of him by an adoption agency which is a local authority.

(2) Subject to paragraph (3), an adoption agency shall require to make an application for an order under section 18(1) of the Act in relation to the child by the end of the period of 28 days from the receipt of a certificate specified in regulation 14(1)(d) certifying that the parent or guardian does not agree with the agency's decision, or from the date that the adoption agency proceeds under regulation 15(2) as though such agreement is unlikely to be forthcoming.

(3) Paragraph (2) does not apply where an application for an adoption order has been made in relation to the child.

Legal process where the child is subject to supervision requirement

18. (1) This regulation applies where a child is subject to a supervision requirement and arrangements for adoption are proposed in respect of him by an adoption agency which is a local authority.

(2) Where an adoption agency decides to proceed under regulation 15 as though such agreement as mentioned is unlikely to be forthcoming, the agency shall within 7 days from the date of the decision notify under section 73(4)(c)(ii) of the 1995 Act the Principal Reporter of this in terms of regulation 12(5).

(3) Subject to paragraph (4), where the adoption agency receives a report from a children's hearing under section 73(13) of the 1995 Act providing advice which supports the decision of the agency in relation to the child concerned the agency, where paragraph (2) applies, shall within a period of 28 days from the date of the children's hearing make an application for an order under section 18(1) of the Act.

(4) Subject to paragraph (5), where the adoption agency receives a report from a children's hearing further to section 73(13) of the 1995 Act which provides advice which does not support the decision of the agency in relation to the child, the agency shall within 28 days from the date of the children's hearing review its decision in the matter and come to a further decision taking into account the report from the children's hearing and any further recommendations from the adoption panel that it may wish to seek and shall notify the Principal Reporter of its decision.

(5) Subject to paragraph (6), where the adoption agency decides further to paragraph (4) that adoption remains in the best interests of the child, the agency shall make an application for an order under section 18(1) of the Act provided that such application must be within the same 28 days specified in paragraph (4).

(6) Paragraphs (3), (4) and (5) do not apply where an application for an adoption order has been made in relation to the child.

Placement for adoption

19. (1) Where an adoption agency has decided in accordance with regulation 12(1) that a prospective adopter would be a suitable adoptive parent for a particular child it shall provide the person proposing to adopt the child with—
    (a) written information about the child's background, parentage, health and mental and emotional development;
    (b) written advice about—
        (i) the need to tell the child about his adoption and origins;
        (ii) the provisions in the Act relating to the right of adopted persons to obtain information from the Register of Births and the availability of counselling services for adopted persons under section 45 of the Act; and
        (iii) the availability of counselling services on any problems relating to the adoption; and
    (c) a copy of a report based on the medical findings on that child obtained under regulation 9.

(2) The adoption agency shall, in connection with the placement of a child for adoption with a prospective adopter—
    (a) notify the local authority in whose area the prospective adopter resides (if different from the agency making the placement) in writing of the placement with particulars of the placement;
    (b) notify the education authority in whose area the prospective adopter resides in writing of the placement with particulars of the placement if the child is of

(a)1980 c.44.

compulsory school age within the meaning of section 31 of the Education (Scotland) Act 1980(a), and such notification shall take place before the placement if the adoption agency's medical adviser considers the child to have a problem of medical significance or special educational needs;

(c) notify the health board in whose area the prospective adopter resides in writing of the placement with particulars of the placement, and such notification shall take place before the placement if the adoption agency's medical adviser considers the child to have a problem of medical significance to his future care;

(d) send a written report of the child's health history and current state of health to the prospective adopter's registered medical practitioner before the proposed placement, together with particulars of the proposed placement;

(e) notify in writing the parents of the child, including where the agency considers this to be in the child's best interests the father or mother of a child who is a parent in terms of section 15(1) of the 1995 Act but does not have parental responsibilities, or the guardian of the child if their whereabouts are known to the adoption agency, that the child has been placed for adoption, but no such notification shall be given to a person who has made a declaration under section 18(6) or 19(4) of the Act (declaration as to no further involvement with the child); and has not withdrawn that declaration under section 19 of the Act;

(f) ensure that the child is visited on its behalf within one week of his placement with a prospective adopter and thereafter on such other occasions as the adoption agency considers necessary in order to supervise the child's well-being as long as the child and the prospective adopter remain domiciled in Great Britain or until an adoption order under section 12 of the Act has been made by the court in favour of the prospective adopters;

(g) ensure that written reports are produced reporting on the said visits.

Progress reports under section 19 of the Act

20. Where parental responsibilities and rights relating to a child who is in Great Britain have been transferred from one adoption agency to another by virtue of an order under section 21 of the Act, the agency from which those parental responsibilities and rights are transferred shall provide such information to the agency receiving the parental responsibilities and rights as it may require to enable it to comply with its duty under section 19(2) and (3) of the Act (progress reports to relevant parent).

Review of case where no placement made within 6 months of freeing for adoption

21. Where a child has been freed for adoption by virtue of an order under section 18 of the Act and the child has not been placed for adoption in accordance with the Act and these regulations after 6 months from the making of that order, the adoption agency to which the parental responsibilities and parental rights are transferred by virtue of section 18 or 21 of the Act shall review that child's case forthwith to determine why no placement has been made and what action, if any, should be taken to safeguard and promote his welfare; and thereafter the agency shall review the case at intervals of not more than 6 months until the child has been placed for adoption.

Provision of information to courts by adoption agencies

22. (1) Where application is made to a court—
    (a) by an adoption agency for an order under section 18 of the Act freeing a child for adoption; or
    (b) by a person proposing to adopt a child and with whom the child has been placed by an adoption agency under the Act and in accordance with these regulations,

the adoption agency shall provide, within such period as may be specified in a timetable drawn up by the court under section 25A of the Act and in accordance with any directions given by the court under that section, a report to the court to which application has been made giving such information on the background and circumstances of the child, his family and (where appropriate) the persons proposing to adopt him as it has been able to discover in accordance with these Regulations and any other matters relevant to the operation of section 6 of the Act (duty to promote welfare of child) as read with section 6A or as may be required by the court in accordance with section 23 of the Act (reports where child placed by agency).

(2) The adoption agency shall also provide to the court to which an application specified in paragraph (1) has been made any report by a children's hearing providing advice on the application obtained in terms of section 73(13) of the 1995 Act or that provision as applied by section 22A(3) of the Act.

Confidentiality and preservation of case records

23. (1) Subject to regulation 24, any information obtained or recommendations, reports or decisions made by virtue of these Regulations or given to the adoption agency, shall be treated by the agency as confidential.

(2) Where a case record has been set up by an adoption agency in respect of a child or a prospective adopter any report, recommendation or decision made by that agency by virtue of these Regulations in respect of that child or that prospective adopter shall be placed on the case record relating to that child or, as the case may be, that prospective adopter, and any case records set up by the agency together with the indexes to them shall be kept in a place of special security.

(3) Subject to regulation 26(2), an adoption agency shall preserve the indexes to all its case records and the case records in respect of those cases in which an adoption order is made in a place of special security for at least 75 years and shall preserve other case records in a place of special security for so long as it considers appropriate; and such case records and indexes may be preserved on computer records or such other system as reproduces the total contents of any such record or index.

Access to case records and disclosure of information

24. (1) Subject to paragraph (3), an adoption agency shall provide such access to its case records and the indexes to them and disclose such information in its possession, as may be required—
   (a) to those holding an inquiry under section 6A of the Social Work (Scotland) Act 1968(a) (inquiries), for the purposes of such an inquiry;
   (b) to the Secretary of State;
   (c) to the Commissioner for Local Administration in Scotland appointed under section 24 of the Local Government (Scotland) Act 1975(b) for the purpose of any investigation conducted under Part II of the Act;
   (d) to the persons and authorities referred to in regulations 12, 19 and 20 to the extent specified in those regulations;
   (e) to a court under regulation 22 to the extent specified in that regulation;
   (f) to a curator ad litem or reporting officer appointed under rules made pursuant to section 58 of the Act (curator ad litem and reporting officer) for the purpose of the discharge of his duties in that behalf.

(2) Subject to paragraph (3), an adoption agency may provide such access to its case records and the indexes to them and disclose such information in its possession, as it thinks fit—
   (a) for the purposes of carrying out its functions as an adoption agency; and
   (b) to a person who is authorised in writing by the Secretary of State to obtain information for the purposes of research.

(3) A written record shall be kept by an adoption agency of any access provided or disclosure made by virtue of this regulation.

(a)1968 c.49.
(b)1975 c.30.

Disclosure of information to adopted person

25. Where an adopted person who has attained the age of 16 years, if in Scotland, or 18 years, if in England or Wales, applies for counselling under section 45(6) of the Act or section 51 of the Adoption Act 1976(a), an adoption agency may disclose information which it has relating to that person's adoption to—

  (a) that adopted person;

  (b) the local authority for the area in Scotland where the adopted person lives, if he has applied to them for counselling;

  (c) the Registrar General for England and Wales;

  (d) the local authority for the area in England and Wales where the adopted person is, if he has applied to them for counselling;

  (e) the local authority for the area in England or Wales where the court sat which made the order relating to the adopted person, if he has applied to that authority for counselling.

Transfer of case records

26. (1) Subject to paragraphs (2) and (3), an approved adoption society may transfer a copy of a case record (or part thereof) to another adoption agency when it considers this to be in the interests of a child or prospective adopter to whom the record relates, and a written record shall be kept of any such transfer.

(2) An approved adoption society which intends to cease to act or exist as such shall forthwith either transfer its case records to another adoption agency having first obtained the Secretary of State's approval for such transfer, or transfer its case records—

  (a) to the local authority in whose area the society's head office is situated; or

  (b) in the case of an approved adoption society which amalgamates with another approved adoption society to form a new approved adoption society, to the new society.

(3) An adoption agency to which case records are transferred by virtue of paragraph 2(a) or (b) shall notify the Secretary of State in writing of such transfer.

James Douglas-Hamilton
Minister of State,
Scottish Office

St Andrew's House,
Edinburgh
24th December 1996

(a)1976 c.36.

SCHEDULE 1 Regulation 3(1)(c)

INFORMATION IN APPLICATION FOR APPROVAL TO ACT AS OR CONTINUE TO ACT AS AN ADOPTION SOCIETY FOR A SPECIFIC SERVICE

1. The adoption society shall specify the following:-

    (a) the nature of the service or services to be the subject of approval;

    (b) the need for such a service or services; and

    (c) how that service or those services contribute to the Scottish Adoption Service.

2. The applicant shall also provide information on the following:-

    (a) the number and qualifications of its staff;

    (b) its financial resources;

    (c) the organisation and control of its operations;

    (d) its procedures for dealing with complaints; and

    (e) if the application is for continuing approval, a record of its activities in the previous 3 years.

SCHEDULE 2   **Regulations 8, 9**

PART I

PARTICULARS RELATING TO THE CHILD

1. Name, sex, date and place of birth and address.

2. Whether the child's father was married to his mother at the time of birth or subsequently. If they have not married, whether he has any parental responsibilities and rights through an order or an agreement.

3. Nationality and race.

4. Physical description.

5. Details of any court orders relating to the child, including residence, maintenance, or parental contact or court orders awarding or depriving any person of the parental responsibilities or rights in respect of the child.

6. Details of any current or previous supervision requirements relating to the child imposed by children's hearings.

7. Details of any brothers and sisters, including dates of birth, addresses, arrangements in respect of residence and contact and whether any brother or sister is also being considered for adoption and, if so, whether it would be in the child's interests to place them together.

8. Extent of contact by all members of the child's birth family, including his father even if he is not married to the mother, and details of any court orders relating to contact.

9. Religious persuasion of the child including details of any baptism, confirmation or equivalent ceremonies and level of current religious observance.

10. Personality and social development.

11. If the child has been looked after by a local authority details (including dates) of placements, including particulars of the persons with whom the child has had his home and observations on the care provided.

12. Names and addresses of schools attended and educational attainments.

13. Any special needs in relation to the physical or mental health of the child and his emotional and behavioural development, and whether he is the subject of a record of special educational needs under the Education (Scotland) Act 1980(a).

14. The child's views in relation to adoption and, if relevant, an application under section 18 of the Act taking into account his age and maturity, including any wishes in respect of his religious persuasion, racial origin and cultural and linguistic background.

15. Whether the child has any right to or interest in any property.

16. Whether an insurance policy for the payment on the death of the child of money for funeral expenses has been effected.

17. A comprehensive medical report signed by a fully registered medical practitioner, including such details as the medical adviser to the adoption agency considers necessary in the circumstances of the child.

18. Any other relevant information which the adoption agency considers may assist the panel.

(a)1980 c.44.

PART II

PARTICULARS RELATING TO EACH PARENT, INCLUDING WHERE APPROPRIATE, A FATHER OR MOTHER WHO DOES NOT HAVE PARENTAL RESPONSIBILITIES OR RIGHTS IN RELATION TO THE CHILD

1. Name, date and place of birth and address.

2. Marital status and date and place of marriage (if any).

3. Nationality and race.

4. Past and present relationship (if any) with other birth parent including an assessment of its stability.

5. Names, addresses and brief details of the personal circumstances of parents of the birth parents and any of the birth parents' brothers and sisters, with their ages or ages at death.

6. Physical description.

7. Personality.

8. Religion, including any wishes in respect of the child's religious upbringing which each parent has in respect of the child's adoption.

9. Educational attainments.

10. Past and present occupation.

11. Whether the mother, if she has parental responsibilities, agrees to the child being adopted and, if not, her reasons for not agreeing.

12. Whether the father, if he has parental responsibilities, agrees to the child being adopted and, if not, his reasons for not agreeing.

13. If the father or mother does not have parental responsibilities in relation to the child whether he or she is intending to apply for, a parental responsibilities order or enter into a parental responsibilities agreement.

14. Whether there is any history of genetically transmissible or other significant disease in the family history of either the father's or mother's family.

15. A comprehensive medical report signed by a fully registered medical practitioner, including such details as the medical adviser to the adoption agency considers necessary in regard to each parent.

16. Any other relevant information which the adoption agency considers may assist the panel.

PART III

PARTICULARS RELATING TO A GUARDIAN

1. Particulars referred to in paragraphs 1-3, 6-10, 15 and 16 of Part II

2. Whether the guardian agrees to the child being adopted, and if the guardian does not agree, his reasons for not agreeing.

PART IV

PARTICULARS RELATING TO EACH PROSPECTIVE ADOPTER

1. Name, date and place of birth.

2. Address.

3. Nationality and race.

4. Whether the proposed adopter has his home in Great Britain and, if not, the address at which he has his home, if different from 2 above.

5. Whether the proposed adopter is domiciled or habitually resident in the UK (i.e. England, Wales, Scotland, Northern Ireland) the Channel Islands or the Isle of Man, and, if not, the country in which he is domiciled or habitually resident. If habitually resident, for how long.

6. If the proposed adopter intends to apply for an order under section 49 of the Act, whether he intends to adopt the child in law or in fact in the country in which he is domiciled.

7. If there are two proposed adopters—
    (a) the date and place of the proposed adopters' marriage;
    (b) whether either proposed adopter has previously been married;
    (c) if so, whether that marriage was dissolved or annulled;
    (d) the grounds for the divorce or annulment;
    (e) whether there are any financial commitments in respect of a former spouse and/or children of a previous marriage.

8. If there is only one proposed adopter, whether that person is married; if so why the spouse does not join in the application, and in particular whether the spouse:-
    (a) cannot be found;
    (b) is separated and living apart, and the separation is likely to be permanent; or
    (c) by reason of physical or mental ill-health is incapable of joining in the application.

9. Details of other members of the prospective adopter's household (including any children of the prospective adopter even if they are not resident in the household).

10. Details of the prospective adopter's parents and any of the prospective adopter's brothers or sisters, with their ages or ages at death.

11. Attitudes to adoption of such other members of the prospective adopter's household and of such of the other members of the prospective adopter's family as the adoption agency considers appropriate.

12. Personality.

13. Previous experience of caring for children and assessment of ability in this respect together, where appropriate, with assessment of ability in bringing up own children.

14. Whether the prospective adopter or any other adult member of the household has previously: -
    (a) notified a local authority of his intention to adopt a child;
    (b) applied to an adoption agency with a view to adopting a child;
    (c) had in his care and possession a foster child within the meaning of section 1 of the Foster Children (Scotland) Act 1984(a) who has been removed under section 12 of that Act;
    (d) been disqualified or prohibited from keeping a foster child under section 7 or as the case may be section 10 of the Foster Children (Scotland) Act 1984 or

---

(a)1984 c.56.

disqualified or prohibited under section 68 or as the case may be section 69 of the Children Act 1989(a) from fostering a child privately;

(e) had in his care and possession a protected child who has been removed under section 34 of the Adoption Act 1976(b);

(f) been convicted of an offence mentioned in Schedule 1 to the Criminal Procedure (Scotland) Act 1995(c) or of an offence under Schedule 1 to the Children and Young Persons Act 1933(d);

(g) had parental responsibilities and rights in respect of one or more of his own children transferred to a local authority under section 86 of the 1995 Act or had one or more of such children made subject to care orders under section 31 of the Children Act 1989(e);

(h) been refused registration as a child minder or worker in a nursery under the Children Act 1989,

and details of any such occurrence.

15. Assessment of ability to bring up an adopted child throughout his childhood.

16. Religious persuasion including the degree of his religious observance.

17. His ability to have regard to a child's religious persuasion, racial origin and cultural and linguistic background.

18. Educational attainments.

19. Past and present occupations and interests.

20. Details of financial circumstances and comments on the living standards of the household.

21. Opinion of adoption agency as to whether any adoption allowance should be considered.

22. Reasons for wishing to adopt a child and extent of understanding of the nature and effect of adoption.

23. Names and address of two referees who are not close relatives who will give personal references on the prospective adopter.

24. Name and address of the prospective adopter's registered medical practitioner.

25. A comprehensive medical report on the prospective adopter signed by a fully registered medical practitioner, including such details as the medical adviser to the adoption agency considers necessary in the circumstances of each prospective adopter.

26. Any other relevant information which the adoption agency considers may assist the panel.

(a)1989 c.41.

(b)1976 c.36.

(c)1995 c.21.

(d)1933 c.12.

(e)1989 c.41.

SCHEDULE 3 Regulation 12(5)

FORM OF REFERENCE BY ADOPTION AGENCY TO PRINCIPAL REPORTER FOR ADVICE BY CHILDREN'S HEARING TO THE COURT

To the Principal Reporter

(Name of adoption agency) as an adoption agency has considered the case of (name and address of child) who is subject to a supervision requirement dated [   ] by a children's hearing for (local authority area), and is satisfied for the reasons set out below that the best interests of (name of child) would be served by the agency [applying under section 18 of the Adoption (Scotland) Act 1978 for an order freeing (name of child) for adoption] [placing (name of child) for adoption]*; and the agency intends to [apply for such an order] [so place (name of child)]*.

The adoption agency has determined that the agreement of a parent to [adoption application under section 16] [freeing application under section 18]* of the Adoption (Scotland) Act 1978 is [likely] [unlikely]* to be forthcoming.

REASONS REFERRED TO
          (insert reasons)

          ....
          (officer of adoption agency)
          (place and date)

*Delete as appropriate

SCHEDULE 4   Regulation 14(1)(a)(i)

MEMORANDUM

ADOPTION OF CHILDREN

This memorandum is addressed to the parent or guardian of a child for whom an adoption application is to be made. This includes the father and mother of a child even though they do not have parental responsibilities or rights in relation to the child. If any part of this memorandum is not clear to you, you should consult the adoption agency (which may be a local authority social work department or voluntary society). You may seek advice from the adoption agency on any matter connected with the adoption of your child, and may also wish to consult your solicitors. This memorandum is intended for guidance only and is not to be regarded as an authoritative interpretation of the law.

1. If the court makes an adoption order, your responsibilities and rights (including financial obligations) as a parent or guardian will be transferred to the adopters and they will become in law your child's parents. You will then have no further right to see your child, unless a condition about continuing contact is part of the adoption order or voluntary contact is agreed by the adopters. You will cease to be the child's parent and will have no right to have your child returned to you.

2. If you wish your child to be brought up in a particular religious faith you should inform the adoption agency. The adoption agency is obliged, however, to make the welfare of the child its paramount consideration. At your request, the adoption agency will be able to tell you if there are any adoption societies which specialise in arranging adoptions with families of a particular faith and it will be able to provide you with the appropriate names and addresses if you wish such a society to arrange for your child's adoption.

3. The adoption agency needs to know whether each of the child's parents or guardian agrees with its decision that the child should be adopted. If you are a parent and have parental responsibilities and rights in relation to the child, or are a guardian, you are asked to complete a certificate (Annex A enclosed) indicating whether you agree or disagree with the adoption agency's decision. Agreement is sought in relation to the adoption agency's decision, and is quite separate from the agreement required by a court (see paragraph 6) in any subsequent application. You should read the certificate carefully, complete Part A or Part B and return it to the adoption agency within 28 days of receipt. This should provide you with sufficient time to take legal advice should you wish to do so. If you agree with the adoption agency's decision, then the adoption agency will make arrangements to have your child adopted. If you do not agree with the adoption agency's decision or do not reply within the 28 days then the agency, if it decides to proceed, will make an application to the court to have the matter resolved - the timescales depend on your child's circumstances, and the adoption agency or your solicitor will be able to advise you of how long this will take. In the event of an adoption application not being possible or appropriate within the timescale required for an application to be made, the adoption agency will apply to the court for an order to have the child declared free for adoption without any further parental involvement. The adoption agency can provide you with further information on this order.

4. If you sign the form of agreement to the agency's decision and your child is subsequently placed with a person wishing to adopt him, then you will not be entitled to have your child returned to you if you change your mind, unless you obtain the permission of the court or the adoption agency. If you do change your mind you should inform the adoption agency at once.

5. Once your child is placed with adopters, they then have to apply to a court for an adoption order. Before making an order, the court will require to know whether you (except where you are a father or mother of the child who does not have parental responsibilities and rights) and any other parent or guardian of the child freely and in full understanding of what is involved, agree unconditionally to your child being adopted. The court will also have enquiries made to check that it will be in the best interests of your child that he should be adopted by the proposed adopters.

6. After the adoption application is made to the court, you will be asked to sign a form of agreement which can be shown to the court as evidence of your agreement. The proposed adopters will either be referred to on this form by a number or they will be named. If they are referred to by a number it will not be possible to tell you who they are. The adoption agency arranging the adoption will explain the reasons for this and will be glad to give you information about the personal circumstances and interests of the proposed adopters and to answer your questions about them as far as possible. Do not sign the form of agreement unless you are willing that your child should be adopted.

7. The court cannot make an adoption order without your agreement unless it dispenses with your agreement on certain grounds. The grounds on which a court can dispense with a parent's agreement are that he or she:-

    (a) is not known, cannot be found, or is incapable of giving agreement;

    (b) is withholding agreement unreasonably;

    (c) has persistently failed, without reasonable cause, to fulfil one or other of the following parental responsibilities in relation to the child—

        (i) the responsibility to safeguard and promote the child's health, development and welfare; or

        (ii) if the child is not living with him, the responsibility to maintain personal relations and direct contact with the child on a regular basis;

    (d) has seriously ill-treated the child, whose re-integration into, the same household as the parent or guardian is, because of the serious ill-treatment, or for other reasons, unlikely.

8. You are not allowed to receive any money for giving your agreement.

9. When an adoption order is made, the Registrar General for Scotland makes an entry in the Adopted Children Register showing the adopters as the parents of your child. A full extract and an abbreviated certificate of the entry in that Register (which takes the place of your child's original birth certificate) can be obtained by the adopters from General Register Office, New Register House, Edinburgh on payment of a fee. When your child reaches the age of 16, he will be entitled to see his original entry in the birth register and to purchase a certificate of entry if he so wishes. This means that when he is 16 he will be able to find out his original names as well as your name and your address when you registered his birth. Should you wish, the adoption agency will discuss with you the implications this may have for you in the future.

CERTIFICATE

TO: (name of Adoption Agency)

I hereby certify that I have received from you a memorandum headed "Adoption of Children" from which I have detached this certificate of acknowledgement and that I have read the memorandum and understood it.

Signature _

Name _

Address _

_ _

Date _

SCHEDULE 5   Regulation 14(1)(a)(ii)

MEMORANDUM

FREEING OF CHILDREN FOR ADOPTION

This memorandum is addressed to the parent or guardian of a child where an application is to be made to the court requesting that the child be "freed for adoption". This includes the father and mother of a child even though they do not have parental responsibilities or rights in relation to the child. If any part of this memorandum is not clear to you, you should consult the adoption agency. You may seek advice from the adoption agency on any matter connected with the adoption of your child, and you may also wish to consult your solicitor. This memorandum is intended for guidance only and is not to be regarded as an authoritative interpretation of the law.

1. If the court makes an order (called a "freeing order"):
    - your responsibilities and rights as a parent or guardian will be transferred to the adoption agency;
    - the adoption agency will then proceed to make arrangements for the child to be placed for adoption as quickly as possible;
    - you will no longer be required to contribute financially to the upkeep of your child;
    - the person wishing to adopt your child will apply to the court in due course and the court, if on investigation considers that this is in your child's best interests, will make an adoption order without being required to consult you first.

2. If you wish your child to be brought up in a particular religious faith you should inform the adoption agency and it will take your wishes into account in selecting new parents for him as far as possible. The adoption agency is obliged, however, to make the welfare of the child its paramount consideration. At your request, the adoption agency will be able to tell you if there are any adoption societies which specialise in arranging adoptions with families of a particular faith and if so it will try to meet your wishes if you wish such a society to arrange for your child's adoption.

3. The adoption agency needs to know whether each of the child's parents or guardian agrees with its decision that the child should be freed for adoption. If you are a parent and have parental responsibilities and rights in relation to the child or are a guardian, you are asked to complete a certificate (Annex B enclosed) indicating whether you agree or disagree with the freeing application being made. Agreement is sought solely in relation to the adoption agency's decision and is quite separate from the agreement required by the court (see paragraph 5) in the subsequent freeing application. You should read the certificate carefully, complete Part A or Part B and return it to the adoption agency within 28 days of receipt. If you do not indicate your agreement within 28 days, the adoption agency will be obliged to make the freeing application to the court within a set timescale determined by the circumstances of your child - the adoption agency or your solicitor will be able to advise you on how long this will take. If you do agree, and the adoption agency places your child with a person wishing to adopt him, then you will not be entitled to have your child returned to you without permission of the court or the adoption agency if you change your mind. If you change your mind, you should inform the agency at once.

4. The adoption agency has to apply to a court for a freeing order. Before making an order, the court will require to know whether you (except where you are a father or mother of the child who does not have parental responsibilities and rights) and any other parent or guardian of the child freely and with full understanding of what is involved, agree unconditionally to your child being adopted. The court will also have enquiries made to check that it is in the best interests of the child for him to be freed for adoption.

5. After the freeing application is made to the court, you will be asked to sign a form of agreement which can be shown to the court as evidence of your agreement. Do not sign

the form of agreement unless you are willing that the child should be adopted and you are also willing to give up your right to be party to the court proceedings when application is made for your child to be formally adopted in due course.

6. The court cannot make a freeing order without your agreement unless it dispenses with your agreement on certain grounds. The grounds on which a court can dispense with a parent's agreement are that he or she:-

    (a) is not known, cannot be found, or is incapable of giving agreement;

    (b) is withholding agreement unreasonably;

    (c) has persistently failed, without reasonable cause, to fulfil one of the following parental responsibilities in relation to the child—

        (i) the responsibility to safeguard and promote the child's health, development and welfare; or

        (ii) if the child is not living with him, the responsibility to maintain personal relations and direct contact with the child on a regular basis;

    (d) has seriously ill-treated the child, whose re-integration into the same household as the parent or guardian is, because of the serious ill-treatment, or for other reasons, unlikely.

7. You are not allowed to receive any money for giving your agreement.

Declaration by a relevant parent

8. You will also be asked to decide whether you wish to be involved in any future questions concerning your child's adoption. If you decide that you do not, the adoption agency will ask you to sign a form declaring this. The form, called a "Declaration by a Relevant Parent", will then be given to the court, so that your wishes will be recorded by the court when the freeing order is made. If you make a "Declaration" you will not be given any more information after the freeing order is granted, and you will not be advised of any outcome of any adoption application. Where you have made a Declaration and subsequently change your mind, you may receive information about your child if you advise the adoption agency in writing.

Your rights if you do not sign a "Declaration"

9. If you do not sign a "Declaration", you have the right to be informed about future developments in relation to your child. It is likely that the adoption agency will tell you as soon as an adoption order is made. The adoption agency must write to you within one year and 2 weeks after the freeing order has been made, to tell you what has happened to your child - whether he has been adopted (if you have not already been told of this) or has been placed for adoption but not yet adopted or is still waiting to be placed with adopters. Thereafter the adoption agency has a duty to continue to notify you of any changes in your child's placement until he is adopted.

10. If the adoption agency has not been able to place your child with adopters within the 12 month period, you have the right to ask the court to revoke the freeing order. The adoption agency can also make such an application anytime after the freeing order is made. If the court agrees to do this as being in the best interests of your child, the responsibilities and rights of a parent are awarded to whoever the court considers most appropriate. Any duties relating to payments towards your child's maintenance which were extinguished by the freeing order will be automatically revived on the date when the court revokes that order.

    During the period when the court is considering your application the adoption agency will not be able to place your child for adoption without the court's permission.

11. If the court does not believe it to be in your child's interests for the freeing order to be revoked, you will not be able to make any further application for revocation unless the court permits this because of a change in circumstances or for any other reason. In such circumstances the adoption agency will continue with its arrangements to find an adoptive home for the child and will not be required to provide you with any further information about his progress or situation.

Birth records

12. When an adoption order is made, the Registrar General for Scotland makes an entry in the Adopted Children Register showing the adopters as the parents of the child. A full extract and an abbreviated certificate of the entry in that Register (which takes the place of the child's original birth certificate) can be obtained by the adopters from General Register Office, New Register House, Edinburgh on payment of a fee. Where the child reaches the age of 16, he will be entitled to see his original entry in the birth register and to purchase a certificate of that entry if he so wishes. This means that when he is 16 he will be able to find out his original names as well as your name and your address when you registered his birth. Should you wish, the adoption agency will discuss with you the possible implications this may have for you in the future.

CERTIFICATE

TO: (Name of Adoption Agency)

I hereby certify that I have received from you a memorandum headed "Freeing of Children for Adoption" from which I have detached this certificate of acknowledgement and that I have read the memorandum and understood it.

Signature _

Name _

Address _

_ _

Date _

SCHEDULE 6   Regulation 14(1)(d)

ANNEX A

PARENT'S AGREEMENT
IN RESPECT OF
PLACEMENT OF CHILD FOR ADOPTION

I

_____

living at

_____

am the mother/father of

_____

who was born on

_____

*A. Agree to my child being placed for adoption and I understand that:

   (a) my child will go to live with adopters as that is in his interests;

   (b) as a consequence of giving any agreement, I will not be entitled to remove my child from the adopters without the permission of the adoption agency or the court; and

   (c) when the court considers an adoption application, it will seek my agreement to the making of an adoption order.

*B. Do not agree to my child being placed for adoption and I understand that:

   (a) should the adoption agency wish to continue with their plan to have my child adopted, they must make a freeing application to the court within set timescales (unless an adoption application has already been made) to have the matter determined;

   (b) in the event of an application for an adoption or freeing order being made, the court will seek my agreement to the making of the order.

Signature ....

        Date ....

*Delete as appropriate.

NOTE:

You should delete either A or B and sign both copies of this form. You should keep one of them yourself in a safe place, and the other one will be kept by the agency. If you change your mind and decide against adoption, you should tell your social worker and your solicitor immediately. Once your child has gone to live with adopters the length of time she or he lives with them may influence the court's decision as to whether it is in your child's best interests to stay there. If you have not already consulted a solicitor you are advised to do so. You should show this document to your solicitor and anyone else advising you.

SCHEDULE 7   Regulation 14(1)(d)

ANNEX B

PARENT'S AGREEMENT TO THE MAKING OF AN APPLICATION TO FREE A CHILD FOR ADOPTION

I

_____

living at

_____

am the mother/father of

_____

who was born on

_____

*A. Agree to my child being the subject of an application under section 18 of the Adoption (Scotland) Act 1978 to have him freed for adoption and for his placement with adopters. I understand that:

   (a) my child will go to live with adopters before the freeing application is made if that is in his interests;

   (b) as a consequence of giving any agreement, I will not be entitled to remove my child from the adopters without the permission of the adoption agency or the court; and

   (c) when the court considers the freeing application, it will seek my agreement to the making of the freeing order.

*B. Do not agree to my child being the subject of an application under section 18 of the Adoption (Scotland) Act 1978 to have him freed for adoption. I understand that:

   (a) should the adoption agency wish to continue with their plan to have my child adopted, they must make a freeing application to the court within set timescales (unless an adoption application has already been made) to have the matter determined;

   (b) in the event of an application for an adoption or freeing order being made, the court will seek my agreement to the making of the order.

Signature ....

                    Date ....

*Delete as appropriate.

NOTE:

You should delete either A or B and sign both copies of this form. You should keep one of them yourself in a safe place, and the other one will be kept by the agency. If you change your mind and decide against adoption, you should tell your social worker and your solicitor immediately. Once your child has gone to live with adopters the length of time she or he lives with them may influence the court's decision as to whether it is in your child's best interests to stay there. If you have not already consulted a solicitor you are advised to do so. You should show this document to your solicitor and anyone else advising you.

EXPLANATORY NOTE
(This note is not part of the Regulations)

These Regulations regulate adoption agencies and make provision *inter alia* for how adoption societies shall be approved by the Secretary of State (regulation 3), their appointment of adoption panels (regulation 7), the functions of the adoption panels (regulation 11) and the duties of adoption agencies in the adoption process.

1996 No. 3257 (S. 247)

CHILDREN AND YOUNG PERSONS

The Adoption Allowance
(Scotland) Regulations 1996

Made	*18th December 1996*
Laid before Parliament	*31st December 1996*
Coming into force	*1st April 1998*

The Secretary of State, in exercise of the powers conferred on him by sections 9(2) and (3) and 51A of the Adoption (Scotland) Act 1978(a), and of all other powers enabling him in that behalf, hereby makes the following Regulations:

Citation and commencement

1. (1) These Regulations may be cited as the Adoption Allowance (Scotland) Regulations 1996 and shall come into force on 1st April 1998.

Interpretation

2. (1) In these Regulations, unless the context otherwise requires—
   "the Act" means the Adoption (Scotland) Act 1978;

   "adopters" means the persons who have adopted or intend to adopt a child or, where there is only one such person, that person;

   "adoption agency" means a local authority or an approved adoption society within the meaning of the Act;

   "adoption panel" means a panel established in accordance with regulation 7 of the Adoption Agencies (Scotland) Regulations 1996(b);

   "attendance allowance" means an allowance under section 64 of the Social Security Contributions and Benefits Act 1992 (c);

   "child benefit" means a benefit under section 141 of the Social Security Contributions and Benefits Act 1992;

   "disability living allowance" means an allowance under section 71 of the Social Security Contributions and Benefits Act 1992;

   "fostering allowance" means the amount of money paid by way of an allowance for a child placed with a foster carer under regulation 9 of the Fostering of Children (Scotland) Regulations 1996(d);

   "income support" means income support under section 124 of the Social Security Contributions and Benefits Act 1992;

   "jobseeker's allowance" means an allowance under section 1 of the Jobseekers Act 1995(e).

(a)1978 c.28; section 9(2) was amended by paragraph 5 of Schedule 2 to the Children (Scotland) Act 1995 (c.36); section 51A was inserted by paragraph 25 of Schedule 2 to that Act.
(b)S.I. 1996/3266.
(c)1992 c.4.
(d)S.I. 1996/3263.
(e)1995 c.18.

(2) In these Regulations any reference to a numbered regulation is to the regulation in these Regulations bearing that number, and any reference in a regulation to a numbered paragraph is to the paragraph of that regulation bearing that number.

Circumstances in which an allowance may be paid

3.   (1) An adoption agency, in making arrangements for a child's adoption, may, subject to paragraph (3) and (5), pay an allowance to adopters where one or more of the circumstances referred to in paragraph (2) exist and if, having decided in terms of regulation 12 of the Adoption Agencies (Scotland) Regulations 1996 that the adoption of the child by the adopters would be in the best interests of the child, it decides after consideration of the recommendations of the adoption panel, that such adoption is not practicable without payment of an allowance.

(2) The circumstances referred to in paragraph (1) are—
   (a)   the adoption agency is satisfied that the child has established a strong and important relationship with the adopters before the adoption order is made;
   (b)   it is desirable that the child be placed with the same adopters as his brothers or sisters, or with a child with whom he has previously shared a home;
   (c)   at the time of the placement for adoption the child is mentally or physically disabled or suffering from emotional or behavioural difficulties such that he needs special care requiring a greater expenditure of resources than would otherwise be required;
   (d)   at the time of the placement for the adoption the child was mentally or physically disabled, or suffering from emotional or behavioural difficulties, and as a result at a later date he requires more care and a greater expenditure of resources than were required at the time he was placed for adoption because of a deterioration in the child's health or condition, or an increase in his age; or
   (e)   at the time of the placement for adoption it was known that there was a high risk that the child would develop an illness or disability and as a result at a later date he requires more care and a greater expenditure of resources than were required at the time he was placed for adoption because such illness or disability occurs.

(3) Notwithstanding paragraph (1) an adoption agency may, after a child has been placed by it with adopters, pay the adopters an allowance if it is satisfied that at the time of the placement one or more of the circumstances referred to in paragraph (2)(c) or paragraph (2)(d) existed.

(4) In each case before an allowance is payable the adoption agency shall require the adopters to have agreed to—
   (a)   inform the adoption agency immediately if—
       (i)   the child no longer has his home with them (or either of them), if they have changed their address, or if the child dies, or
       (ii)   there is any significant change in their financial circumstances or the financial needs or resources of the child; and
   (b)   complete and supply the adoption agency with an annual statement of their financial circumstances and the financial circumstances of the child.

(5) An allowance may be paid from the date of placement for adoption or from such later date as may be determined by the adoption agency and notified to the adopters.

Amount of the allowance

4.   (1) The allowance shall be of such amount as the adoption agency determines in accordance with paragraphs (2) and (3).

(2) In determining the amount of allowance the adoption agency shall take into account—
   (a)   the financial resources available to the adopters (including in respect of the child any financial benefit which would be available to them after adoption but excluding in respect of the child disability living allowance and attendance allowance payable and, where the adopters are in receipt of income support, child benefit);

(b) the amount required by the adopters in respect of their reasonable outgoings and commitments (excluding outgoings in respect of the child); and

(c) the financial needs and resources of the child.

(3) The allowance paid by the adoption agency shall not include any element of remuneration for the care of the child by the adopters and in any event may not exceed the amount of the fostering allowance (excluding any element of remuneration in that allowance) which would be payable if the child was fostered by the adopters.

Procedure in determining whether an allowance should be paid

5. (1) Subject to paragraphs (2) and (3), an adoption agency shall, before an adoption order is made in respect of a child whose adoption it is arranging or has arranged—

    (a) consider whether an allowance may be paid in accordance with paragraphs (1) to (3) of regulation 3;

    (b) supply information to the adopters about allowances including the basis upon which amounts of allowances are determined;

    (c) give notice in writing in accordance with paragraph (4) to the adopters of its proposed decision as to whether an allowance should be paid and the proposed amount, if any, which would be payable;

    (d) consider any representations received from the adopters within the period specified in the notice;

    (e) make a decision as to whether an allowance should be paid, determine the amount, if any, which would be payable and notify the adopters of that decision and determination.

(2) The adoption agency shall not be required in a case to which regulation 3(2)(d) or

    (e) of these Regulations applies, to determine the amount of an allowance unless or until—

        (i) there is a deterioration in the child's health or condition, or an increase in his age (in a case to which regulation 3(2)(d) applies); or

        (ii) the onset of the illness or disability (in a case to which regulation 3(2)(e) applies),

and as a result the child requires more care and a greater expenditure of resources than were required at the time at which he was placed for adoption.

(3) An approved adoption society which holds itself out as not being an adoption agency which normally pays allowances shall not be required to comply with sub-paragraphs (a) and (b) of paragraph (1) and need comply with sub-paragraphs (c), (d) and (e) of that paragraph as respects any adopters only if it has considered whether or not to pay an allowance to those adopters.

(4) A notice under paragraph (1)(c) shall state the period of time within which the adopters may make representations to the adoption agency concerning the proposed decision or determination and the adoption agency shall not make a decision or determination under paragraph (1)(e) until after the expiry of that period.

Information about allowances

6. After a decision has been made to pay an allowance, the adoption agency shall notify the adopters in writing of the following:—

    (a) the basis of the determination of entitlement to an allowance and of the assessment of the amount of the allowance;

    (b) the amount of the allowance as initially determined;

    (c) the date of the first payment of the allowance;

    (d) the method of payment, the frequency of payment and the period of payment of the allowance;

(e) the arrangements and procedure for review, variation and termination of the allowance under regulation 7.

Review, variation and termination of allowances

7.   (1) The adoption agency shall annually review payment of an allowance having first received from the adopters a statement setting out the adopters' address and whether the child still has a home with them (or either of them), the adopters' then current financial circumstances and the then current financial needs and resources of the child; but in any event the adoption agency shall review the payment of allowance if it learns of any material change in the circumstances of the adopters or the child, including any change of address of either.

(2) Subject to paragraph (6) where the adopters fail to supply the adoption agency with an annual statement in accordance with their agreement under regulation 3(4)(b), the adoption agency may suspend payment of an allowance until such time as a statement is supplied.

(3) The adoption agency may vary or suspend payment of the allowance if, as a result of a review, it considers that the adopters' need for it has changed or ceased since the amount of the allowance was last determined.

(4) Subject to paragraph (5) the adoption agency shall terminate payment of an allowance when—

   (a) the child ceases to have a home with the adopters (or either of them);
   (b) the child ceases full-time education and commences employment or qualifies for a placement on a Government training scheme;
   (c) the child qualifies for income support or a jobseeker's allowance in his own right;
   (d) the child attains the age of eighteen; or
   (e) any period agreed between the adoption agency and the adopters for the payment of the allowance expires.

(5) Notwithstanding paragraph (4)(d) the payment of an allowance may continue beyond a child attaining the age of eighteen for so long as the child continues in full time education and has not reached the age of twenty one.

(6) Where payment of allowance is suspended in terms of paragraph (2) the adoption agency may recommence payment and may pay arrears after a statement is supplied.

Confidentiality, preservation and access to records

8.   (1) Subject to regulation 24 of the Adoption Agencies (Scotland) Regulations 1996(a) any information obtained or recommendations received or decisions made by virtue of these Regulations shall be treated by the adoption agency as confidential.

(2) The adoption agency shall place a record of the details of each allowance in respect of a child including details of any determination under regulation 4 and review under regulation 7 on the case records that it is required to set up under the Adoption Agencies (Scotland) Regulations 1996.

James Douglas-Hamilton
Minister of State,
Scottish Office

St Andrew's House,
Edinburgh
18th December 1996

(a)S.I. 1996/3266

EXPLANATORY NOTE

(This note is not part of the Regulations)

These Regulations make provision in respect of adoption allowances schemes prepared by adoption agencies to pay allowances to persons who have adopted or intend to adopt a child in pursuance of arrangements made by such agencies. These new schemes are to replace the existing schemes approved by the Secretary of State under section 51(5) of the Adoption (Scotland) Act 1978 which are to be revoked on the coming into force of sections 51A (adoption allowances schemes) and 51B (transitional provisions as respects adoption allowances) of that Act as provided for in paragraph 25 of Schedule 2 to the Children (Scotland) Act 1995.

The Adoption Allowance Schemes Direction 1996

The Secretary of State, in exercise of the powers conferred on him by section 51A of the Adoption (Scotland) Act 1978(a) and of all other powers enabling him in that behalf, hereby gives the following Direction—

Citation and commencement

1.   This Direction may be cited as the Adoption Allowance Schemes Direction 1996 and shall come into force on 1st April 1997.

Period for preparation and publishing of plans

2.   The period within which each local authority which is an adoption agency shall prepare an Adoption Allowance Scheme under section 51A of the Adoption (Scotland) Act 1978 for the payment by the adoption agency of allowances to any person who has adopted or intends to adopt, a child in any case where arrangements for the adoption were made, or as the case may be are to be made, by the adoption agency shall be one year commencing on 1st April 1997.

N. G. Campbell
Under Secretary,
The Scottish Office

Edinburgh
27th December 1996

(a)Section 51A was inserted by the Children (Scotland) Act 1995 (c.36), section 98(1) and Schedule 2, paragraph 25.